# Fixing Up Motorcycles

*Also by LeRoi Smith*

How to Fix Up Old Cars

Make Your Own Hot Rod

# FIXING UP
# MOTORCYCLES

*LeRoi Smith*

ILLUSTRATED

DODD, MEAD & COMPANY

NEW YORK

# Contents

190011

# Contents

# Introduction

America has adopted the motorcycle. A form of transportation and sport long considered alien to the American frame of mind has literally overwhelmed the population, exploding on all fronts at once. Motorcycles are everywhere: on the turnpike, in the school parking lots, weaving their way through downtown traffic, inching along a remote mountain trail. They have, in essence, become the horse of the modern American "frontier."

The motorcycle isn't new to the United States. As in European countries, it was one of the early forms of vehicle experimentation, ideally suited to the backyard inventor with an idea and no investment dollars. Compared to the automobile, it remains low-budget although total expenditure for a custom or racing bike can reach into the thousands. A drag-racing motorcycle, for example, can be built for under $3,000, while a competitive four-wheeled dragster will run upwards of $40,000. A Bonneville hot rod streamliner can seldom be built for less than $30,000, even when the owner does much of his own work, yet New Zealand's Burt Munro annually comes to the American salt flats with a motorcycle streamliner that cost less than $2,000. Unable to afford high-compression pistons, he made special molds in the beach sand and cast his own. Ingenuity, then, is the essence of motorcycling.

Until 1960, however, motorcycles were never a household word in America. The Harley-Davidson and several years ago the Indian were the American bikes, and both were more a function of police work than everyday pleasure. There were the usual "motorcycle nuts" in every town, a very few people who enjoyed two-wheel transportation, often distinguished by a tight-fitting black leather jacket, high-topped engineer boots, and the famous "Harley" hat. This was the way of things in most areas, but Southern California was different.

A long-established hotbed of mechanical innovation, Southern California has the unique geographical structure of immense deserts. Almost no people live in these remote regions, thus there are practically no fences. Cross-country travel then is restricted only by the terrain itself. While hot rodders were utilizing desert dry lake beds for high-speed car racing, motorcyclists were discovering the thrill of cross-country desert racing.

Through the years, special motorcycle clubs grew in and around Los Angeles, with seldom a weekend passing without a scrambles or hare-and-hound event somewhere. It is estimated that fewer than 4,000 enthusiasts participated in these off-road competitions, but that number remained relatively constant through several decades.

In the Southwest these enthusiasts became a motor-cycling elite, a position often reserved for the more hardy of any sport. And they were proving a fantastically valu-able testing ground for motorcycle manufacturers. In Europe, where motorcycles were king and motorcycle de-signers were considered superior to American designers, the primary test facilities for a new bike idea were road races and off-road trials. However, the American deserts were far more demanding than the majority of European courses, and with a weekly total of nearly 2,000 riders thrashing machines, the Southwestern deserts became proving grounds.

While the heavy, and bulky, Harleys and Indians were used on the desert, competition success gradually shifted to the lighter-weight and easier-to-control English imports. The Triumph and BSA and AJS soon pushed the American machines from the sagebrush. The Harley was still around, but only where pure, brute horsepower could win, as in hillclimbs or oval track racing.

As desert riding finesse improved, the demand for still lighter-weight machines created a bevy of new backyard motorcycle designers. A slightly different frame, an im-proved fork, modified engines or seating—anything that would help a winning rider could create a manufacturer.

But for the most part, these design improvements found their way into factory production motorcycles. The rider then had only to make minor adjustments to suit his particular skill and style of riding. Before long, the Greeveses were challenging the invincible Triumphs.

While all this attention was being given traditional four-stroke-powered motorcycles, some revolutionary changes were being made to the two-stroke engine. Hardly a new idea—the two-stroke principle is as old as the internal combustion engine—the two-stroke had begun to receive attention from large international manufacturing firms. Considerably less expensive to produce than the four-stroke engine, the two-stroke is also much lighter. It had been long used in motor scooters and various low-performance motorcycles. Suddenly the design was beginning to produce power. And along came Honda.

The resurgence of the Japanese economy following World War II, a direct result of imagination, international influence, and government subsidy of business, had created a gigantic manufacturing capability. Low-cost transportation being vital to Asian nations, Japanese builders embarked on motorcycle construction without fanfare. To the rest of the world, and especially American enthusiasts, the Japanese were building nothing more than motorbikes.

In the late 1950s Honda Motor Company decided to import their line to the United States. But to encourage sales, they would have to include a tremendous advertising campaign to acquaint the American buyer with the advantages of a motorcycle. With a sharp eye to the economic climate of the United States, Honda came on strong. A vast network of dealers was established, supported by national advertising, a type unknown to motorcycle enthusiasts in California or Maine. "You meet the nicest people on a Honda," became as well known a phrase as Yankee Doodle, and the lightweight Honda caught on.

Americans were gaining more and more leisure time, and were turning happily to all forms of outdoor recreation. The Honda promised heretofore unavailable access to lands previously reserved for hiking and horseback riding. At the same time, the small Honda and similar imports were not as difficult to ride as the big Harley or the powerful Triumph. America was learning to ride a motorcycle.

Honda opened the vast American market to motorcycling. Where most smaller towns had never before had a motorcycle dealer, every hamlet and village came to support two or three franchises. Gradually the emphasis shifted from a simple lightweight Honda to a special-duty trail bike. Dad, mom, and the kids could buy a motorcycle especially suited to their own skills (or lack of skill) and all could hustle off to the mountains for a weekend vacation.

While Honda sold America on the motorcycle, other imports sold the idea of a two-stroke. Back in the desert, a few riders were beginning to experiment with lightweight chassis powered by hopped-up two-stroke engines. At first, these bikes were outclassed by the "heavies," and a special lightweight class allowed them to race among themselves. But things began to change. Soon, the Ring-Dings (so named because of the unique exhaust noise from a two-stroke engine) were outrunning the heavies and the latter classification became the minority. Development of off-road racing lightweights has gone hand-in-hand with improvement of both trail and street bikes until the contemporary motorcycle is considerably better than its ten-year-old counterpart.

The success of Honda stimulated Harley-Davidson (the single surviving American motorcycle manufacturer) to diversify their line. Considered something of a stuffy fuddy-duddy, H-D had continually improved the venerable 74 as a highway machine, and had begun production of the Sportster as a lighter-weight, smaller displacement "sports" model. This design was placed on the market well before the Honda invasion but was never intended as a lightweight in the general sense. Even Harley-Davidson was surprised at the success of the Sportster, with brisk sales and a high resale price. Sportster became *the* road bike for an enthusiast who wanted performance and a modicum of riding comfort.

With the rash of imports flooding the country, H-D countered with imports of their own, brought in under the Harley name, but this finger in the dike reaction has failed to stem the flow of international names. Students now banty names like Bultaco, Husqvarna, and Yamaha as they once did Mustang, Charger, and GTO. The motorcycle has become a very tangible part of American life.

While the specialty motorcycle is very popular, it still makes up a minor portion of total bike sales. For the most part, the motorcycle is regarded as a utility vehicle, and as such must see duty under all conditions; street, trail, and occasional competition. When the weather is agreeable, the motorcycle becomes a practical "third car" for the family. It is low-cost transportation for student and office worker alike. Statistics reveal a tremendous jump in the number of motorcycle registrations by state since 1968, with over 6 million motorcycles licensed by 1970. Since the motorcycle does not make it to the junkyard as rapidly or regularly as the automobile, it is estimated there will be over 20 million motorcycles on the highway by 1975.

The used motorcycle then becomes commonplace, which lowers the cost of transportation for anyone willing to fix up a secondhand bike. It is possible for the mechanically ept enthusiast, teenager, or senior citizen to build a personal bike for under $100! A ridiculously low sum it would seem. But suppose a nonrunning lightweight is purchased for $25 (not at all uncommon). Parts are inexpensive, and if the enthusiast can detour the $8- $10-an-hour charge for professional help, he can ride for almost nothing.

The used motorcycle has helped create the tremendous surge in custom bike interest. The question is often asked whether or not custom motorcycles, or choppers as they've come to be known, aren't just a fad. They are as much a fad as the hot rod, which was invented two days after the automobile and is still around. Choppers were always around, but not in the numbers now common. Some fantastic business success stories have evolved from the chopper industry, an industry still infant. Tom McMullen, hot rod enthusiast for years, built his first chopper in 1967. When friends asked for duplicate parts, he gathered a few high-school-age neighbors to make the parts in his home garage. One month later he was in a rented store, and three years after that was grossing over $5 million a year in custom parts sales. He had started the highly successful *Street Chopper* and *Hot Bike* magazines and by 1971 was able to establish special accessory parts testing procedures, with results supplied to state departments of motor vehicles for future equipment laws.

The motorcycle has become as American as apple pie and Steve McQueen.

# Fixing Up Motorcycles

# What Is a Motorcycle, Anyway?

If you were to ask an international motorcycle designer exactly what a motorcycle is, you'd likely get a string of technical terms a block long. And he'd end up by saying something like, "In the end analysis, a motorcycle is a two-wheeled, self-propelled vehicle." Almost correct. But there are three-wheeled, self-propelled vehicles that are motorcycles, for example the traditional motorcycle with a sidecar, or some of the old designs with two front or two rear wheels. In fact, the fastest motorcycle in the world is over thirty feet long, weighs several tons, and has gone over 600 mph at the Bonneville Salt Flats. Craig Breedlove's land-speed-record "car" was not a car at all . . . it was a motorcycle because it only had three wheels. The international motorcycle-record governing body, the FIM (Federation Internationale Motorcycle), recognized the three-wheeled jet car, that is, motorcycle, several years ago and the record still stands.

Even the word *motor* is something of a misnomer. If we were to follow our English instructor explicitly, we'd call the motorcycle an enginecycle, motor being the definition of an electrical power device. Way back in grandpa's day, or before, the motorcycle became what it is when someone mounted an internal-combustion engine in a bicycle chassis. At that time it would have been correctly called a motorbike, such a term referring specifically to the chassis rather than to the engine. The motorbike is still with us in great numbers, manufactured primarily by overseas plants as a ready means of economical transportation for a great number of people.

In fact, during the very early days of motorcycling, the machine was often referred to as the "poor man's automobile," a term it really does deserve in some ways, but does not deserve in others. While a modern small-displacement motorcycle may cost only a few hundred dollars, a large road bike may cost more than an automobile.

The first motorcycle, or motorbike, predates the first automobile by some years, simply because the earliest attempts at an internal-combustion engine were best suited to something like a bicycle. These early engines were reasonably small, and produced a minimal amount of power at best. The bicycle required very little power (on a hill the rider would pedal to help the engine over the hump!), and combining the two was something most any small-town tinkerer could do. In the early 1800s there were even experiments with steam-powered bicycles, products that were grotesque in every form.

The bicycle chassis began to be upgraded during the late 1800s, as the engines improved and rider demands for a more sturdy vehicle grew. By the early twentieth century, motorcycles were being used for ordinary transportation, competition, sporting rides, and even as commercial delivery vehicles. Then, as now, they were less expensive to purchase, easy to maintain, and required very little gasoline.

The very first motorcycle was patented by Gottlieb Daimler of Germany in 1885. This utilized one of the internal-combustion engines he had also invented, and the machine looked like a very large wheeled bike with short wheelbase and training wheels. The same man was involved with starting the automobile company now called Mercedes-Benz. It is interesting to note that Daimler introduced a V-twin engine way back in 1889, which was even air-cooled like the majority of modern motorcycle engines. As can be imagined, the early Daimler motorcycles were unusual in every respect. Although Daimler had also invented the carburetor, getting one of the pioneer engines to run smoothly at all rpm's was an almost impossible task. Final drive was by a belt from the engine crankshaft directly to the rear wheel, with a kind of idler pulley that would tighten or loosen the belt at the rider's command. There was no springing, and seeing such a device being ridden on dirt roads must have been humorous. But it was the beginning.

During this same time in the late 1800s, another German motorcycle was being worked on with a design that would let the rider place both feet on the ground to steady the machine when it was not moving. Built by the firm of Wolfmueller & Geisenhof of Munich, this design was something like a step-through girl's bicycle, but had the engine connecting rods linked directly to the rear wheel, like a steam locomotive. The 2-horsepower engine was claimed to go as fast as 24 mph. While engines of the period were all of fractional horsepower (as compared to today's bikes) they provided enough power for the frames of the period. Engine location was tried everywhere, from over the front wheel to behind the rear wheel to below the frame.

While all this motorbike inventing was going on in Europe, an American named Hedstrom was working with powered bicycles as pace vehicles for racing bicycles. Hedstrom and a man named Hendee formed a manufacturing company in 1901, and the Indian motorcycle was born. These early Indians were famous for simplicity of engine and the controls were on the handlebars. Of course, there were many other motorcycle manufacturers in the United States at this period, among them the famous Merkel and Pope names. The New Era did away with the traditional pedals and included a two-speed transmission.

The early engines of around 2 horsepower were enough for the bicycle, but soon heavier frames were being constructed, which meant more powerful engines were necessary. With everyone and his uncle inventing a motorbike it wasn't long before a great deal of experience had been amassed by builders on both sides of the Atlantic. The next phase of motorcycle design came into being, starting in the early 1900s and running through the late 1920s. For want of a better title, I'll just call this the Antique era, as compared to the motorbike era just described.

These new motorcycles were beginning to take on the appearance of a modern bike, with longer wheelbase, sprung front suspension, improved brakes, hand controls on the handlebars (as well as some foot controls), and frames designed to accommodate the engine and all its necessary accessories, such as fuel and oil tanks. Like their four-wheeled counterparts, these motorcycles look very much alike to the untrained eye, and except for significant engineering variations, they were indeed similar. And as with the early cars, the smaller companies fell by the wayside. To many middle-aged Americans, the only motorcycle names they can recall are Indian, Hendersen, and Harley-Davidson.

The economic slumps of the early 1900s and the Depression of the 1930s teamed to restrain motorcycle popularity in America. Tight money meant few frivolities, and the motorcycle had unfortunately gained the reputation as a plaything, something the rich person kept around for personal riding thrills. Increased power and performance had outstripped available paved highways, and in the early days the motorcycle as a pure off-roader was not to be considered. Finally the motorcycle gained an image it did not fully deserve: "If you want to kill yourself, get a pistol or get a motorcycle!" There were no safety helmets back then, and protection was usually no more than a leather jacket and knee-high boots. In this condition of mechanical limbo the motorcycle was to remain, at least as far as the general public was concerned, until the current revival of interest in the late 1950s.

Today, there is a motorcycle for practically every riding need, leading many enthusiast families to have several different types of bikes. There are the road machines, such as the Harley 74, Honda 750, big-displacement Kawasaki, BMW, etc. There are the off-road, or "desert" bikes, which now range in displacement size from 125 cc through the largest engines available. There are trail bikes, which are a kind of multipurpose off-road machine, and even a new series of vehicles called ATV, which stands for all-terrain vehicle. These are usually scaled versions of mini-bikes with three very large tires for flotation on any kind of marginal surface. In between are the midi-bikes, the mini-cycles, the mo-peds, etc., etc., etc. The motorcycle has become a very specialized piece of mechanical equipment.

## The Road Bikes

The off-road motorcycle has made cycling popular across this country, but the road bike will give the sport strength in coming years. While economy has been the great lure to most buyers of foreign motorcycles, versatility has been the key to sales success in America. Dad gets a kick out of chugging around through the open woods, mom likes the sense of accomplishment which comes from learning to ride, the kids have found motorcycles ideally suited for school transportation. This dual-duty type of requirement has cast the majority of motorcycles in the role of base transportation more than recreational vehicles. The bike may be ridden hard on the weekend, off-road or on trails, but it may get twice the mileage on city streets during the week.

It is inevitable that anyone introduced to any form of motorcycle will eventually end up riding a road bike. It makes a great mount for city trips, and recently there has been a surge of interest in the road bike as an answer to large-community traffic problems. A businessman with briefcase and suit in a safety helmet on a run downtown on his Yamaha is now a common sight. The road bike has become the third "car" for many families.

While the only real definition of a road bike would be any motorcycle that is used primarily for hard surface riding, it is generally agreed within the industry that a road machine is one of larger displacement. That is, the engine is powerful enough to sustain open highway speeds without laboring. A Honda 350 might be perfect for zipping around town, but it would be marginal for a really comfortable cross-country journey. The Honda 500 or 750 would be much better for extended tours. Essentially, then, the road bike is powerful, docile in traffic, stable at high speeds, equipped with excellent brakes, and comfortable. From the very beginning, this has been the criteria for such machines.

The Indians and H-D's produced just before and after World War II were powerful, heavy, and great for a ride from Los Angeles to New York. The imported Triumph and BSA and similar "lightweights" were not nearly so comfortable on long trips. The United States did not have a monopoly on the road image, however, since the German BMW with shaft drive was considered by many to be the very epitome of road comfort.

It was a design standard to include a large, well-padded, and spring-mounted seat on these earlier road motorcycles. The reason was simple: there was often no rear suspension on the motorcycle and the seat had to take up the shocks. Harley-Davidson and Indian bikes became famous for their oversize seats, which were large enough for a passenger. During this era, which is best described as that of the "rigid" bike (which refers to the rigid frame with no rear suspension), the road rider was easy to spot. He invariably wore a small billed cap and a giant leather belt kindly referred to as a "kidney belt." The machine vibrations coupled with road shocks transmitted through the unsprung frame meant sustained trips without some kind of back support was almost impossible. When the rear suspension was added to make motorcycles handle better, it had the

8

side effect of eliminating the need for kidney belts. The modern road bike is far more comfortable than its counterpart of 1950.

While the great emphasis these past several years has been on off-road motorcycles—an emotional reaction by the enthusiast rather than a consideration of anything practical—the road bike is making giant strides in sales. There are several organizations that cater to these road-oriented riders, such as the AMA (American Motorcycle Association) and the IFOA (International Four Owners' Association, primarily a gathering of Honda four owners). Smaller groups are around for the enthusiast who works with a specific type of road machine, such as CAMA (Classic and Antique Motorcycle Association), Norton Owners Club, etc. The way to find out about any of these organized groups is through local motorcycle shops and monthly motorcycle magazines.

Concern of these organizations is usually some form of road activity, such as tours by AMA, conventions by CAMA, and so on, but all have a common goal in seeing that motorcycle legislation on either local or national level is not detrimental. A great deal of motorcycle legislation is introduced into state and national channels every year. It is the responsibility of organized groups to review and to support or oppose these laws.

The road bike must pass all state laws relative to vehicle equipment, an area where the new rider may find trouble when he buys a used vehicle. If you're buying a used bike and aren't sure whether or not it complies with current laws, ask a motorcycle shop to pass judgment. Even ask a highway patrolman if no experts are available. The new road bike will undoubtedly have all the requirements, which may range from separate stopping system for front and rear wheel to turn signals spaced a certain distance apart.

## Dirt Bikes

Any off-road motorcycle can most properly be called a dirt bike, although this might be confusing if a trail bike is being considered. The accepted definition for dirt bike is any motorcycle used extensively for off-road sport riding and/or off-road competition. Essentially, the dirt bike is a very high performance vehicle, and is not necessarily restricted to just two wheels. There are a growing number of dirt machines equipped with side hacks for class racing, these three-wheelers already going the distance in such grueling endurance contests as the Baja 1000 and the Mint 400. Use of the extra wheel is not peculiar to America, however, since side cars have long been used by European riders for winter off-road activities. The third wheel seems to improve bike handling when the going is slick.

Dirt bikes come in every possible size and shape, from the tiny 50-cc motorbike to the huge Harley 74. In days past, it took something of a giant to handle the big Harley in the desert, one of the reasons the smaller English imports were so popular. The new generation of fast lightweight two-strokes has almost eliminated the big bikes from serious off-road competition, and now it has become an almost weekly battle between two-stroke manufacturers to stay on top of the heap. All this competition has bred tremendous improvements in the lightweights, improvements that can be immediately introduced in factory models since the production numbers are so limited. End result of all this updating is an extremely varied and versatile line of off-road equipment.

If a person were to select a motorcycle strictly upon prevailing popularity, he would undoubtedly be led to purchase a dirt bike in preference to a road machine, although the road bikes are coming on strong now that powerful two-stroke engines are available. But by and large, the off-road motorcycle remains the sales leader in most states. In some respects, this popularity is a bit misleading, since many bikes are really selected for dual-purpose use; highway during the week and off-road on the weekend. Eventually, however, the trend shows most of these dual duty machines end up as off-road transportation only.

Because there are so many different motorcycle manufacturers, especially those making two-stroke machines, and because these manufacturers are relatively low-volume producers (in terms relative to automobile production), there is an almost weekly change in sales leaders. For a long while it was Honda, then came Yamaha, then Suzuki. Next came Hodaka and Maico and Husqvarna. The reason for the fluctuation in sales was simply the results of weekly competition events, particularly those held in the vast Southwestern deserts. Tabloid newspapers are avidly read by riding enthusiasts, so when a particular brand of motorcycle starts winning big, a swing is under way to that mount. While this change in brand names may effect only a few of the hard core riders, it does have a marked effect on sales. For instance, if the local "hot shoe" happens to switch from brand X to brand Y, every enthusiast in the area knows, and they also know he did it primarily to stay competitive. Keeping up with the pack, then, is the key to survival in motorcycle production ranks.

Because most motorcycle factories are quite small, with a very limited amount of tooling, it is possible to make running changes in any particular model at a reasonable cost. At the same time, while many factories have a considerable number of staff engineers, the majority of manufacturers rely on experience gained at competition events. Thus it is that a slight change in an engine exhaust system may gain that very vital 1 horsepower, which in turn is the difference in winning or losing. Without doubt, there has been more improvement in the motorcycle during the last ten years than in the previous forty years. Much of this improvement can be laid directly to the dirt bike.

The quality that most sets the dirt bike apart from the typical highway machine is controllability. In years past when most motorcycles were great monsters of weight, the off-road rider was at the mercy of the machine. He went where it went. Now, with the emphasis on extremely light weight, the rider has become all-important. How he positions his weight on rough terrain and through corners has an immediate and direct bearing on how the bike will cover that surface. The rider has thus become the imperative missing link in motorcycle performance, something like the jockey in horse racing. While a particular rider might do well on a specific dirt bike, he might be poorly suited to a different type of bike. It becomes a matter of fitting the rider and his riding style to the bike.

As mentioned, light weight is the most distinguishing factor about a dirt bike, with great emphasis upon stronger-but-lighter frames, better tires, just-right handlebars, etc. But the engine has played an immense role in the current popularity of the dirt designs. The four-stroke engine is smoother, and is claimed to be more foolproof by its advocates, but the fact remains that the two-stroke is almost single-handedly responsible for the great success of off-road bike use. The two-stroke is simple, so that home repairs are inexpensive, and the basic construction of such an engine lends itself well to the kind of heavy abuse encountered in off-road activities. At the same time, engineering improvements in the two-stroke have raised its performance level to that of the four-stroke, correcting one of the early faults of two-stroke powerplants. Generally, the lightweight bike with a two-stroke will require a different riding technique in off-road use than for the four-stroke (it does not have the gutsy low-end torque), but

**13**

once mastered the two-stroke is extremely responsive.

As a rule, any bike that is being transported by trailer or rack on an automobile can be expected to rest under the title of dirt bike, while those motorcycles ridden long distances would be titled road bike.

## Track Bikes

As might be expected, there are a number of motorcycles that are neither road nor dirt. I refer here to the racing motorcycles, machines created and used only for racing. In this classification would be the road-type machine which is used for long distance road racing (on courses identical to sports car races). For the off-road bike there is the enduro machine and the motocross design, sophisticated improvements on the basic dirt bike. Then there are the drag bikes and the highly specialized land-speed-record machines. All these, however, are take-offs on the original motorcycle.

Special, race-only motorcycles are as old as the motorcycle itself, fitting every category just listed as well as a few peculiar classifications that have long since died away. Oval track motorcycle racing has been popular in America for many decades; road racing has been the proving ground for European motorcycle builders since the turn of the century; land-speed-record attempts go back to early runs on poor highways and not much better beaches; drag racing is really just a modification of the English "sprints" popular in the 1930s. The change has not been in the sport, but rather in the machine.

Oval track racing takes on two specific forms in the United States. The most commonly known is "flat-track," or bike racing on fairground horse-racing ovals, and is essentially nothing more than using a motorcycle over the same course as that used by cars (midgets and sprints). For many years this was considered the epitome of motorcycle sport in America, and the riders were regarded as only slightly less than supermen. A similar form of oval racing takes place on a much shorter track, and is called Speedway. This is really a kind of wind sprint, where a small number of riders go flat out for a few laps around a very short course. However, except for a brief time before World War II, Speedway racing has been limited in the United States. It is now making a great return, although about the only motorcycle used is the Jawa. Interestingly, Speedway bikes use no brakes and have wide "longhorn" handlebars reminiscent of older motorcycles, this in direct opposition to the flat-trackers.

There is one bit of history in American motorcycling that warrants mention. Hillclimbs came into vogue just before and after World War II, when owners of large-displacement Harleys and Indians found that trying to top a steep incline was great fun. And exciting. For nearly two decades it was not uncommon to find a hillclimb of some kind featured in nearly every community in the country, or at least those towns that could find a hill tall enough and steep enough to be a test. While there are still an isolated few hillclimbs of this sort, that phase of motorcycle sport has largely disappeared.

A specialty act among the off-road bikers would be the motocross event, something that has been gaining popularity in America the last ten years. Motocross is a form of closed-course racing over an uneven surface, including sand and water obstacles. It is quite like the American form of desert racing, but whereas the desert courses may have individual laps of twenty miles or more, the motocross course is restricted to a few acres. It is better suited to spectator control, and thus is a popular form of motorcycle competition for a promoter to feature. Recently automobile racing tracks of all kinds that have hilly terrain have been adding motocross courses, and topflight European riders are appearing in several American events. The motocross is virtually the exclusive domain of the super-lightweight two-strokes.

The all-American version of the motocross has been around for years now, and is more aptly called The Desert. With millions of desert acres available to Southwestern bike riders, it is no wonder that hare & hound and enduro desert events should have become so popular. Unlike the European countryside, which has a shortage of public area, the American desert stretches to the horizon, without a fence and often without a road for hundreds of miles. Southern California motorcycle clubs were quick to realize the usefulness of this situation and introduced courses designed to take the rider far afield over nearly impassable terrain. Such a course may be short, two or three laps of ten or fifteen miles each that can be covered in part of a day. Other courses are considerably longer and require two or even three days to cover.

In either case, the course is marked with splotches of lime, which means the rider must navigate the course without becoming lost as well as try for the fastest possible lap speeds. Because of the very great distances involved with desert racing it does not have the crowd appeal of the motocross, and it is not profitable for a promoter, but it is motorcycle riding at its best for the riders. In desert riding the individual's number plate signifies how he has finished in the previous year's point standings, thus the number 1 plate means that rider won the most points, and so on down the line. Merely to be a number 250 out of 3,000 participants is a singular honor. Riders are also divided into classes according to expertise, but all enthusiasts ride a race at the same time.

Because of the sheer numbers often involved in a desert race (upwards of 1,500), starting a race becomes something of organized chaos. Bikes may be lined up abreast for nearly half-a-mile, sometimes two or three bikes deep. Well into the distance ahead, usually on a small hill, a smoke bomb or large pennant is used as the starting signal, at which time all riders race for the single trail that marks the course. Obviously there is a great deal of dust and confusion.

Sometimes just as confusing, but seldom dusty, is the road race. This is the premier form of motorcycle racing, and by far the most dangerous. Courses may be specially made for the purpose, such as Daytona, in Florida and LeMans in France, or they may be sections of ordinary highway roped off for the purpose. The latter courses are the most difficult, since daily traffic will have worked the asphalt surface into rough washboards and chuck holes, and in Europe those streets within a small village will be cobblestone.

The road-racing bike will fit into several different engine displacement categories, and will have special sidecar classes. In all cases, light weight and maximum horsepower are desirable. Because these machines can easily hit 150 mph, the slightest slip in riding technique can send a rider sprawling. At the same time, finesse in riding form and perfect balance are so well honed that bike champions often make the move to sports and racing cars very successfully. The road-racing motorcycle almost always utilizes new manufacturing ideas that eventually find their way into production.

Drag racing is really something of a new character, especially on the American scene. Sprints over a two-way course have been common in England for years, but the shorter quarter-mile American course has only recently come into its own. Motorcycles have raced on car drag strips since 1949, but not until the great general interest in bikes during the late 1960s did drag-strip organizers give serious thoughts to all-bike competition.

During the early days of American drag racing it was not uncommon for a finely tuned Harley to outdrag a hot rod, but that was largely a dead issue by 1955. Motorcycle drag racing became the art of a very tiny group for the next fifteen years, part of this group in Southern California, the other part on the East Coast. Finally, during the mid-1960s, these builders began to receive factory production engines capable of producing great horsepower. The new Honda four, and highly modified Harley Sportsters began putting out more horsepower than available tires could transfer to the asphalt. Late in 1969 an automotive drag tire builder experimented casually with motorcycle "slicks," and bike drag speeds jumped dramatically. As this is written, exotic "fuel-burning" motorcycle dragsters are over 180 mph with an elapsed time in the 8-second range. With further tire and engine development it is possible the 200-mph barrier will be broached within a year or two.

The loneliest spot in the motorcycle sport just has to be the land speed racer. Racing all alone on a vacant expanse of Utah salt flat, the LSR rider runs only against the clock —a clock that computes how long it took to drive through a measured mile and then reads this out of the timer as ultimate miles per hour. Like the English sprints, this is a two-way race, since a wind factor must be considered. The average of the two-way run is the final top speed reached. And it is an extremely difficult speed to reach.

Except in the classes below 200 mph, most LSR bikes are far indeed from the typical run-to-the-store variety sold for street use. Like the dragsters, LSR bikes are usually stretched in wheelbase until they may be as long as a passenger car. A spidery framework of spindly tubing may support one, two, or more engines, often as not behind the rider. In some cases the rider is astraddle the framework, but more often he will be seated in a semireclining position similar to that in racing cars. The sum of this effort will be encased in a fiberglass or aluminum covering looking like the drop tank from an airplane or a giant cigar. The desired effect is maximum streamlining, since it takes horsepower to overcome wind resistance, and every little bit of horsepower is good for more miles per hour. The current world record of 265 mph is held by Cal Rayburn.

Although it wouldn't seem to be a motorcycle, the three-wheeled jet cars that ran 600 mph in the late 1960s were officially listed at motorcycles, since a car must officially have four wheels to qualify for the automotive land speed record.

When you sum it all up, a motorcycle is many different things in one. But something it is not is a mini-bike or motorbike. The motorcycle comes closest of any form of man-made surface transportation to giving a feeling of total freedom of movement. What it will become in the next fifty years is unknown, but we do know one thing . . . it will definitely be exciting!

---

# How to Buy a Motorcycle

Somehow, it's a very special day when you go for that first motorcycle. A kind of time when you get that secret wish, when you finally break the restraints of convention, when you "splurge" for a piece of equipment you may not really need. At least, the motorcycle has traditionally been a kind of "toy" to Americans. Fortunately, that image is going by the way. The motorcycle will be many things to anyone who owns it, but for the young person who may select a motorcycle as his very first method of transportation, it is an excursion in self-expression and responsibility. The idea is to buy your first motorcycle wisely, both in selection of the actual bike and in choosing the method of payment, then to care for that investment with respect.

Almost no one but the buyer will be in favor of a motorcycle purchase. Somehow, way back in years past, the idea of a motorcycle seemed to set any person well apart from the crowd, the picture being a slightly cocky fellow with mustache, leather helmet, high-top boots, and a devil-may-care silk scarf thrown to the wind. Surely anyone who would ride a motorcycle would also fly a stunt plane, drive race cars, and hurtle over Niagara Falls in a barrel, all for an afternoon's lark.

While it isn't quite such a stumbling block to own a motorcycle now, all the other problems of pre-purchase remain—what kind of machine to buy, how many cylinders, which type engine, how large a displacement, should it be for cash or should it be financed, what about insurance? The names change, the times change, the problems do not.

Probably the first thing to take care of is the decision as to the kind of engine that will be most desirable. This means will you want a two-stroke or a four-stroke. No one can give you a concrete answer on this; you must become involved with motorcycling and then gradually lean toward the type of engine that best suits your riding habits.

The basic difference in the two engines is the manner of fuel induction and burning. The four-stroke engine must pull the intake mixture into the engine as the piston goes down in the cylinder. On the next upward stroke this mixture will be burned and the expanding gases will drive the piston downward on a power stroke. As the piston starts back up, the exhaust valve opens and the piston pushes the burnt gases to atmosphere, then on the succeeding down stroke the fuel mixture is pulled into the cylinder again. This means there are a great number of mechanical pieces moving just to keep valves, pushrods, rockers, and lifters in time with the piston. It also means the four-stroke engine will tend to have a kind of heavy power stroke every other time the crankshaft revolves 360 degrees.

The two-stroke was designed to do away with all the mechanical units for induction and exhaust of the four-stroke. When a piston moves upward in a closed cylinder, it compresses the fuel mixture. The same thing happens when the piston moves downward, although the crankcase area below the cylinder is a much larger area than the combustion chamber and will not have as great an air density. Two-stroke engineers felt that by using this crankcase pressure they could force the fuel mixture into the engine without valves. If this can be done, the fuel can be fired on each stroke, instead of every second crankshaft revolution. It means a far smoother running engine, one of the basic differences between the two- and four-stroke designs. You'll have to ride a Honda four and a Harley V-twin to appreciate this smoothness.

The two-stroke engine design has been around for years, but not until the mid-1950s did it really get a boost from motorcycle engineers. Early problems of overheating and lubrication have been worked out. At the same time, the four-stroke has been sophisticated to the point where its inherent strength and dependability are becoming secondary to maximum power production.

The two-stroke will require more general maintenance

than the four-stroke, but it is such a super-simple design your grandmother could do a top-end job while baking bread. The four-stroke will get slightly better gas mileage, but will be heavier and harder to overhaul. It's a toss-up right now as to which design is better. You'll just have to study the characteristics of both and choose accordingly.

Another problem is that of cylinders: how many and how? If you're going to be doing off-road work of any kind, you can vote in favor of the single cylinder, whether two- or four-stroke. For some reason the strong power stroke of a single is often better suited to dirt use than any of the multi-cylinder engines, perhaps because a multi will tend to break the rear tire loose too easily. The singles do well on the highway, but they are not as common as the multis.

Twin cylinders have been around for ages, whether in V-twin or side-by-side arrangement, whether canted or vertical or opposed. They are powerful in all displacement sizes, and the relatively small engine size means lower total vehicle weight. If a single engine style were to dominate the street motorcycle, the twin would be in.

Coming on strong, however, are the new triples, in canted or vertical form. Finally, there are the fours, such as those fantastic 15,000-rpm machines introduced to road racing so successfully by Honda. But the more cylinders, the more sophisticated the engine, whether two- or four-stroke. The three- and four-cylinder engines are almost exclusively destined for road use, although some are popular with drag-racing and land-speed-record bike builders.

You'll have to decide, before you buy, just what kind of riding you will be doing. At the same time, you'll have some of the decision made for you by the prices; the less complicated the engine, the less expensive the bike.

If you're going to ride any off-road areas at all, you might want to select a bike that is designed as a dirt machine. There is a tricky thing in motorcycle design called frame neck angle, and this angle, combined with the type of front end, wheelbase, etc., determines to a great extent just how well the bike will handle. The typical street machine (which might be advertised as good for occasional off-road stints) will probably have steering that is too responsive, too quick for off-road comfort. The dirt bike that can be ridden on the street would be the better choice. But at the same time, the street bike might have brakes that are better for high speeds and that give better traction on a hard surface. Keep this in mind when buying.

There is the question of bike size, too. If you're going to do mostly hard-surface riding, you don't want a flea-weight that blows over from the wind of a passing truck, and you already know that most states require a minimum 15 horsepower for any vehicle using freeways (that means nothing less than 125 cc). The 250 would probably be a good, all-purpose vehicle if you don't know whether you'll be off-road or on, while the 175 might be more to your taste if you're definitely going off-road. The big motors, those over 250, are for either expert handlers in the dirt, or a person who wants to do a lot of long-distance highway work in a modicum of comfort.

The brand of machine you buy is going to be dictated largely by your experience, or inexperience, in motorcycling. If all you've heard around the neighborhood is how keen a Yamaha is, a Yamaha you'll buy. Your consideration should be made on more concrete ground, though. Is there a reputable dealer handy? Are the parts reasonable (is the bike in good supply, or rare)? What is the selling price of used Brand X as compared to Brand Y? Which seems to be holding its resale value better? On and on and on. The best possible advice I can give is to shop patiently and carefully, weigh the facts, then decide.

If you have friends with motorcycles, ask for some demonstration rides on their various bikes. This will give you a good initial idea of what to expect in different types of motorcycles. All the while, you should be attending local bike meets, watching how different riders handle their machines, and learning about your local dealer. Do not ever be afraid to check the credentials of a dealer; even dealers will urge this bit of common-sense shopping. A fly-by-night operator can open a hole-in-the-wall motorcycle shop, sock it to a dozen or so unsuspecting customers, and be gone before nightfall. You might want that Brand X bike badly and learn later that the dealer has the reputation of loading repair bills. Okay, you buy a bike from the man, but after a couple of visits to his facility you end up doing your own repairs. Harsh, but the facts of life. Same situation exists in sports cars . . . a rear-end universal joint for a Jaguar XKE costs $25 from the Jag dealer and $4.95 from the Ford dealer. Same part, both made in America. Get the picture?

Whether the dealer is one of the unscrupulous few or the dependable many, you should start motorcycle ownership expecting to do much of the maintenance yourself. A motorcycle is really a straightforward mechanical contraption, and it can be the source of hours of tinkering pleasure for the most rank amateur mechanic. But don't work on any motorcycle without the proper mechanic's manual. You can get this manual from the dealer, and you should read it through several times during the first few weeks of new bike ownership. At the same time, the small owner's booklet you get at time of purchase will give vital information on vehicle care. It is imperative that you read and obey this booklet.

Any time you buy a new motorcycle, whether you are an experienced old hand or a newcomer, listen to what a reputable dealer might suggest. Remember that you are selecting from quite a range of motorcycle types—scramblers, street-scramblers, road machines, enduros, trials, and trail —and within each manufactured line there will be perhaps as many as twenty-five types. Currently, there are over thirty-five different manufacturers, so the choice is going to be difficult at best.

Remember that caution about buying a bike designed for something you'll never experience, like a scrambler for riding to school? Same thing goes for buying a machine that is too small for you. Most new riders will tend to select their first bike on the factor of appearance; it looks small enough to handle and the engine doesn't look too powerful. The dealer will most likely suggest a motorcycle that seems just a bit too big and powerful. But he is working from experience, and he knows that most new buyers tend to buy a machine that is too small. When this happens, the new rider will master the motorcycle within a few days of purchase and then be unhappy that he cannot make the trade for a bigger unit immediately. You'll be happy to know that most good bike dealers have an informal training program for new riders, and all new riders should take advantage of one.

Incidentally, while you're looking the dealer over, check his parts supply well. If he sells more than one brand of bike, does he stock a good supply of parts for all brands? Since the newcomer isn't likely to really know what the parts supply situation might be, he will probably have to rely on what other cyclists in the area advise. This is where the new owner can really get some invaluable information. Don't be bashful when around motorcyclists. If there is a group of riders congregating somewhere, make it a point to approach them with questions as to new bike purchase and parts supply from a specific dealer. They will be happy to share their information; after all, they had to start, themselves, and they know the problems you may be facing.

The question of financing should be answered before you waste time at any dealership. Some dealers, particularly the larger ones, will have a good arrangement with a local bank. Other very large and long-established dealers may carry their own financing. The smaller dealers will often work with finance companies. If you can arrange for your family bank to handle the financing prior to shopping for a bike, that's best. If you're under the state legal adult age eighteen or twenty-one, your parents must sign for the financing. At any age, you'll want to consider the financing charges carefully.

Most bikes that fall into the category a new rider might select will have a new price tag ranging from $900 to $1,500. This is not a very large amount compared to the price of a new automobile, and consequently very long-term financing is not avalaible. Two and three years' financing is average. However, the rate of interest charged will vary greatly—8 and 10 percent are rather common rates charged by banks, but 12 to 16 percent can be expected from some finance companies. Should there be a problem arranging personal financing—which is not as uncommon as it might seem (some new buyers with outstanding credit advise that while they can arrange financing on a $5,000 automobile at the finest terms, they encounter difficulty getting financing for a motorcycle at all)—you might use a small loan company with a rate as high as 20 percent or more. Obviously, with high rates of interest it is best to finance the lowest amount possible. Accessories for riding, such as clothing and helmet, and even bike-modification accessories should not be included in financing.

Insurance is another question each and every motorcycle owner should be concerned with. The young rider is going to pay far more for insurance than the older rider (over twenty-five) when it comes to automobiles, but this is not necessarily the case with liability insurance on motorcycles. The smaller the bike, in terms of cubic-inch displacement, the lower will be the liability insurance rates. A 100-cc bike can cost as low as $15 per year, or it can cost upward of $50, depending upon where you live. It is quite possible to pay either twice as much or half as much as a rider in a neighboring city. Although rates seem to be set at the whim of local insurance officials, never ride, even for one mile, without liability insurance.

Some kind of comprehensive insurance, such as fire, theft, and so on, will be considerably more expensive, so much so that it is often questionable whether this type of insurance is worth while. For example, in some states it will cost almost $350 per year for comprehensive insurance on a motorcycle valued at $700! Obviously, two years' worth of insurance costs as much as the motorcycle, so in two years your motorcycle has cost you $1,400 instead of $700, and each year it will become still more expensive. California police organizations report that nearly 90 percent of all stolen motorcycles are never recovered, because the unit is usually disassembled and sold for parts. This is an extremely high ratio of nonrecovery. Faced with this kind of theft, as well as the very high cost of comprehensive insurance, the motorcycle owner must decide either to accept the insurance or to take special care of his vehicle.

There are many new electronic anti-theft devices being marketed through motorcycle shops, and any person who plans on owning a motorcycle (with or without insurance) should install such a unit. The insurance rates are so high because of the theft problem; if everyone cooperates in reducing theft, the rates will hopefully be reduced. Preventing the theft in the first place seems the best solution.

During all your running around and checking out new motorcycles, it is also a good time to talk to the "old hands" about a riding school. You can learn to ride on your own, taking the lumps as they come, or you can get some short-cut pointers from riders who've already been there. Sometimes your teacher might be the finest rider in the county and still not be able to show you a thing. It all becomes a matter of listening to many different riders explain how they approach the problem, then being selective as to what approach will work best for you. At the same time, you might be lucky enough to have a special motorcycle riding school in your area.

Riding schools are sometimes sponsored by local dealers. Certainly, if a dealer sells you a motorcycle he will give you the very basics of riding. But this is not enough. Some larger manufacturers have instituted special riding programs through various dealers, the programs usually scheduled on a weekend and staffed by both dealer personnel and local expert riders. These have been excellent sources of riding instruction so far, and are highly recommended. In other cases, local motorcycle clubs have taken on the job of holding classes periodically, and these, too, are very well attended. In the absence of any type of school, a few enterprising new riders have approached their local police department motorcycle officers for assistance.

If you can't find help from anyone, it is best to contain your new-found enthusiasm for the time being to some large lot. Start by "pre-flighting" the machine. Learn where everything is, and how to operate all foot and hand controls before the engine is started. Test the balance while the motorcycle is motionless, and note how the bike will become "heavier" as you lean it too far to one side. Roll the bike back and forth, using hand and foot brakes, and note how the bike reacts to each brake. Swing the steering from lock to lock and test the handlebar "feel" with the bike at rest. All this will change as the motorcycle moves, of course, but it is essential to really know a machine in order to ride it well.

Never start the motorcycle in gear wtih the hand clutch lever pulled. It is very easy to engage the clutch accidentally, and you may end up in a tree before you ever get started on your riding lesson. Take the bike out of gear. You will have decided when buying the machine whether you wanted an electric or kick start. There is no denying that one of the things that has made motorcycling so popular is the introduction of the electric starter. If you are slight of build, chances are good you'd have a very hard time starting a large-displacement motorcycle engine—there is just too much compression to overcome. Some bikes, particularly Harley-Davidson, have a magneto system that requires some healthy kicks of the starting lever. Enthusiasts overcome this problem by installing high-performance magnetos, but an electric starter is even better.

With the engine running and the transmission in neutral, test the throttle-grip response. Some bikes will have a very light throttle spring, others quite heavy. Some engines will take the gas quickly, others sluggishly. When you've figured about how the engine will respond, depress the clutch lever, put the transmission in low gear, and slowly let out the clutch. Chances are good that a bike with normal gearing will idle away from standstill without your increasing the throttle setting. An engine that has been modified will be practically impossible to move without very careful coordination of clutch slippage and throttle manipulation.

Ride the bike in low gear at slow speeds, turning first one way and then the other. After a while you will be able to do this slow riding without removing feet from the pegs. Interestingly, the better you become at slow riding, the better you will be at speed. Gradually increase speed, still in low gear, and practice stops and starts until all maneuvers are smooth.

**33**

Now start in low gear and shift to second, while turning and going in a straight line. Practice downshifting from second to low, since using engine compression to aid in braking is a sure sign of a professional rider. Go on through all the gears, with increasing speeds, until you have confident control in all turns and speed changes. When you feel you really know how to ride a motorcycle, it is time to beware!

A great majority of motorcycle accidents occur to new riders just at the point when they feel they have mastered their machines. The professional will tell you a person never really does master a motorcycle. To get some of this enthusiasm out of the blood, go to an off-road area to practice. First, make some runs on a flat dirt surface, and learn how the bike will slide at varying speeds and in different types of turns. Then progress to hills and rough terrain. In an amazingly short time you will decide that perhaps the best way to ride a motorcycle is to be continually awake, aware at all times to the responses necessary on the rider's part to control the vehicle. When you reach this state, you're ready to learn how to ride a motorcycle. From here on, it is a matter of practice.

---

# Fixing Up the Used Bike

If you have any kind of ability with simple hand tools, most used motorcycles can be made to run as well as when they came off the showroom floor. Common sense and a few tools are all that's needed for most minor repairs, and many jobs that look difficult will turn out to be a couple of evenings' easy work, provided you approach the subject with a little forethought.

If you didn't do it at the time you bought the bike, make a list of all the things that need repair or replacement. Divide the list into two parts, those things that you feel sure can be done at home, and those that will have to be done by a repair shop. In most cases, the number of things that can be done in the garage with the tools at hand will be much larger than the list of items which will require professional help. Common items that will need fixing on most used bikes are missing bolts or washers, loose or bent spokes in the wheels, and control cables that are worn and need to be replaced. Electrical troubles are common on bikes that have been sitting for long periods of time, and the battery (if the bike is equipped with one) may have to be replaced.

The handiest piece of home repair equipment a new owner can have is the shop repair manual for his bike. If you didn't get one with the bike, drop by a dealer that handles the model you purchased. The cost of most manuals is only a few dollars, and they're well worth the money. The shop manual is different from the little book that comes with the bike when it is sold new. That book only provides information about a few basic service points. The shop manual is larger, and has detailed information on everything from overhauling the engine to special tools that may be required to perform certain jobs. The many photos and drawings will include step-by-step instructions on disassembly, repair, and reassembly of every part of the bike. Many of the repair jobs that a new rider would normally spend money to have done at a shop can be done at home with a shop manual.

When working on a bike, there are some simple shop rules to follow that will save time and money. Keep the work area clean. Many of the moving parts of the motorcycle engine, transmission, and running gear can be harmed if dirt or grit is allowed to get inside. Make sure the correct tools are on hand when the job is started. Nothing is more frustrating than to get halfway through a job and find that you don't have all the tools needed to finish the job. The same goes for new parts. Unless the correct replacement parts are on hand, taking the bike apart won't help you much.

Another good rule to follow when working on a bike is to take things apart with a system. Instead of pulling parts out of the bike and just tossing them on the bench, set them aside in order so that you can put them back correctly. If you think you can't remember which way you took something apart, and the shop manual doesn't show that particular step in detail, write it down. You'll find that laying everything out in a planned manner will increase your ability to tackle things that are usually done by repair shops.

Before you actually start unbolting things from the bike, take a few minutes to give it a thorough cleaning. This will make it a heck of a lot easier to work on, and may reveal some things about the bike's condition. If you're at a loss as to just how the cleaning should be done, try this. Take the bike to the local two-bit carwash and give it a complete going over. The hot water and detergent used in car washes will not harm the bike; the whole thing works like a cheap steam cleaner. Be careful to dry out the bike thoroughly after the wash. Condensation can cause all sorts of electrical troubles.

While you're drying the bike, look it over for such things as loose fenders or missing mounting bolts. Run your hands across the spokes in both wheels to see if any of them are loose or bent. The rims should be inspected for obvious dents or cracks in the metal. Check the valve stems where they protrude from the wheel rim by bending them to one side, and looking for signs of weather checking or cracks in the rubber. This will give you an approximate indication of the condition of the inner tubes.

Some dirt bikes will have a couple of threaded stubs with bolts on them sticking through holes in the rear rim. These are attached to a curved piece of metal that holds the tire in place when the bolt is tightened. This keeps the tire from slipping on the rim and tearing the valve stem off the tube. Some of the knobbie tires used in the dirt really grab the ground, and sudden use of the throttle can spin the tire on the rim if these rim locks are not used. Make sure the bolt is tight; loose ones can cause trouble.

While checking the rear wheel, look at the exposed teeth on the rear sprocket. The sides of the teeth should be straight. If they are curved or show signs of obvious wear, better add a new sprocket and chain to your list. Replacing the sprocket without installing a new chain won't help much. The bad chain will just eat up the teeth on the new one.

Also check the rear shock absorbers for any signs of leaking. This might not be too apparent right after the bike has been cleaned, but if you sit on the bike and bounce up and down a few times, the shocks will expand and contract. Any really bad leaks will show up as a light film of oil around the rubber seal.

When you get the bike home, block it up on something so that both wheels can be turned freely. This will give you a chance to check both wheels for alignment. If the wheel shows any perceptible wobble when it is spinning, it will have to be trued. This is a job that can be done at home, but the cost of having them trued and balanced by an expert is low, so unless you want to do it for the experience, take them to a shop.

While you are spinning the wheels to check for alignment, listen to the wheel bearings. Any rattling or clicking sounds can mean dry or worn bearings. These should be checked, and lubricated or replaced depending on how badly they are worn. Look at the nuts holding the axle onto the forks and swingarm. Stripped or damaged threads indicate that the previous owner didn't take very good care of the bike and those parts may have to be replaced.

The tires themselves are something that should be checked. Look them over for cuts and weather checking. Tires that are worn dangerously should be replaced, especially on street bikes. A tire intended for off-road use only can still be good even though it looks partly worn out. As long as there is about ⅛ or ¼ inch of the knobby portion of the tire left, it should give good service until you can afford to buy new tires.

Tires on road bikes will sometimes show much of their wear on the sides of the tread rather than in the center. This indicates the former owner considered himself something of a road racer. If much of the tread is worn down, change them for new tires. When a road bike is leaned over in a fast turn, it really needs all the tread it can get.

The front suspension is next on the list. Check it for leaking just as you did the rear shocks. Sit on the bike and bounce it as hard as you can to compress the front forks. Sometimes it helps to enlist the aid of a friend to add his weight to the project. Look at the area just above the rubber dust shield on the lower fork legs for signs of oil leaking. A very light film of oil on the upper leg in the shiny area where the dustcap rubs is all right. If there is a lot of oil seeping around the cap, the forks will have to be disassembled and serviced. The shop manual will provide a step-by-step procedure for this.

While you and your buddy are bouncing the forks up and down, listen for any sound that might indicate lack of oil in the forks or worn sliding parts. Front forks that have been allowed to run dry will have no dampening effect, and can cause some interesting (and sometimes scary) things to happen to the bike on uneven terrain. After you are satisfied that the fork hydraulic action is satisfactory, there are several things to examine on the upper part of the forks.

The upper fork legs are held in alignment with each other by a pair of metal plates called triple clamps. The legs are fastened in holes in the triple clamps with bolts that squeeze the clamp around the leg. Check these bolts to make sure they are tight. At the point where the front fork assembly fastens to the frame, there is a shaft supported in the neck of the frame by bearings. These bearings are often worn badly in a used bike that has seen a lot of rough service, and extra play can add to any handling problems. To check this, prop the bike up so that the front wheel is off the ground, then grasp the forks and shake them firmly. Any extra play in the forks will be easily seen. The amount of free play can be adjusted by tightening or loosening the large nut on the top of the stem. If there is considerable play, the bearing may be worn out and need replacing.

One part of checking a used bike that I can't stress enough is a complete examination of the wiring. Trying to fix the electrical system of a used bike can be hard for the beginner if he doesn't have a little background in how electricity works. I won't try to teach any electrical theory here, but there are some basic things that can be checked quickly to tell the source of most problems.

Look closely at all the wiring. Probably half the failures in motorcycles are wiring problems. On most bikes the seat is hinged to allow access to equipment located underneath it. A lot of the wiring runs through this area, and the battery is located here on most bikes. Inspect very carefully each wire that you can see. Look for places where the wiring may be rubbing against the frame or other metal objects. Check all connectors of the push-together type to make sure they are not loose. If you don't have the tools to install new connectors on the ends of wires, but have a soldering gun handy, solder loose connections solid. It might take you a few minutes to remove at a later date, but you'll stand a better chance of not being stranded in the middle of the desert with a dead bike.

A roll of electrical tape will be a big help in reducing the problems of chaffing or wearing of wires where they pass through holes in sheet metal. The same holds true for areas where constant rubbing on frame or bodywork has worn through insulation. Don't use regular friction tape that is sticky on both sides. The stuff doesn't adhere to the plastic insulation worth a darn! The rule of thumb to follow here is, if it looks the slightest bit worn, tape it. Tape is cheap insurance against wiring failure.

After you have looked over the wiring under the seat (we'll get back to the battery later), follow the main bundle forward under the gas tank to where it leaves the frame to go to the headlight shell. You may want to remove the gas tank if the coil is located under it, and in some cases there are connector boards under the tank as well. The shop manual will give you the procedure of removing the tank, and it will give you a chance to check the tank for leaks or dents on the underside and in the channel where it fits over the frame. On most bikes, the wiring bundle running under the tank is already wrapped with tape or is inside a plastic sheath. This area seldom gives any trouble until you get to the part that runs from the frame to the forks. This part of the wiring bundle must flex every time the forks are turned. It can stand inspecting even if the tape must be removed to let you get a good look at the wiring.

Almost all motorcycles use the space behind the headlight, inside the headlight shell, as a connecting point for all control wiring running to the lights, starter (if the bike is equipped with an electric starter), horn, and anything else that is controlled by the rider. Take the headlight out of the shell and examine the connectors behind it for loose or worn plug-ins and look for frayed wiring. If you find a couple of wires that don't seem to be connected to anything, don't worry too much, they may be for equipment that is not installed on your particular bike.

After a complete inspection of the wiring, if the bike has an electrical problem, try the obvious first. It's surprising how often the battery will prove to be the culprit even if the bike will run after a fashion. Most motorcycle batteries are designed so the water level can be checked from the side. Check to see that the battery is not dry. This is a common problem with bikes that have been sitting for a while.

If the battery is not dry and shows no signs of being cracked or other problems, take it out and have it checked. When you remove the battery, always unhook the ground connection first. This will prevent accidental completion of the circuit while removing the power-carrying cable, and shocking yourself or damaging the battery. On most bikes the battery is marked with two signs to show the positive (+) and negative (−) posts. Normally the negative post will be hooked to the ground side of the circuit, but some bikes use a positive ground system, so check to see that the lead you are disconnecting is routed directly to the frame or other metal surface.

Another way to recognize the ground cable is that it is usually made out of flat braided wire and has no covering over it. The cable carrying power from the battery to the rest of the circuit will be covered to prevent its being shorted out against the frame or other metal parts. With the ground cable unhooked, the power-carrying cable can be disconnected without fear of causing an arc.

After the battery is removed, check it over for physical signs of trouble. If the case was fully enclosed and you couldn't check the water level while the battery was still in place, check it now. A completely dry battery is ruined, and maybe another sign that the previous owner neglected the bike. Broken or cracked batteries are trouble. Battery acid leaking from a broken battery can corrode aluminum parts or destroy wiring. Check the battery box or the support the battery rests on for signs of leakage. It will show up as white powder or crystals. One of the things most often forgotten is that battery acid will cause burns on hands and exposed parts of the body, and can eat holes in clothing. Be careful when handling a leaking battery.

Take the battery to a shop and have it tested with the proper equipment (you can't tell anything about the electrical condition of the battery by just looking at it). If the battery is good, reinstall it in the frame and try each of the electrical functions on the bike. Any items such as turn blinkers or indicator lights that do not function are probably a simple matter of bad bulbs or loose connections.

If the bike won't start, and you're fairly sure that the electrical system is good, there are only two other basic symptoms to check. The first is fuel. If the engine isn't getting enough gas and air, it won't run no matter how good the rest of the bike is. The first thing to check on any bike that won't start is the spark plug. Remove the plug (or plugs) and check to see if it shows any signs of raw fuel. If it is completely dry, chances are, something is wrong in the carburetor or gas line. Don't overlook the obvious, it may be something as simple as an empty gas tank. If there is fuel in the tank and you have not forgotten to turn on the fuel valve located underneath the tank, then something may be blocking the line. Shut the fuel off, then disconnect the line at the carburetor inlet fitting. Stick the end of the line into some type of container (a baby-food jar works fine) and turn on the gas. If nothing comes out, either there is some kind of sediment in the tank blocking the line, or just possibly the tank vent in the gas cap is blocked. Usually if the vent is blocked, the gas will run for a few seconds and then stop.

If there is a good flow of gas from the line and the spark plug stays dry when the engine is turned over and the throttle is operated, then most likely there is something wrong inside the carburetor. A sticky float or a jammed needle and seat can cause this. Remove the carburetor and give it a cleaning and rebuild just as you would the one on a car. One thing that may be different: don't be too surprised if the parts man tells you there is no carburetor kit for your bike. Many bikes don't have a kit and you have to order the replacement parts separately.

If the plug turns up wet with fuel but nothing happens when you kick the engine over, there is a good possibility there is no spark. Reconnect the plug to the wire and lay it on the head so that the electrode of the plug is close to the head. Crank the engine over. If the ignition is putting out any power, the spark will jump from the plug to the cylinder head. If nothing happens, you have an ignition problem and will have to refer to the shop manual to fix it.

The third thing that must be present is compression. If there is sufficient fuel and a strong spark, and the engine still will not start, there may be a broken ring or something else that is preventing the cylinder from holding compression. To check this, put one finger over the spark-plug hole and crank the engine over. If the pressure buildup tends to force your finger off the hole, there is enough compression and the problem is somewhere else. Remember, this is a rough check for compression. Even with enough compression to move your finger off the hole, there can still be a problem with the rings or piston that could cause the engine to run poorly.

If a quick check of the condition of the engine in your bike locates a problem, then you are ready to sit down with the shop manual, because you have just passed beyond the

*Cycle Guide*

The traditional straight-up-and-over American hillclimb is not as popular as it once was, but the challenge is as great as ever. This cyclist is about to lose it.

Very popular in the west are Enduros, long off-road bike races that stress driver endurance and bike dependability. Enduros are excellent training grounds for tougher, closed-course races.

RIGHT: The small displacement two-strokes have a place in road racing, but competition is fierce and driver finesse must be at a maximum.

ABOVE: Flat track and TT racing are similar. TT courses are winding like road-racing courses, flat tracks are oval, both are usually dirt. Here the bike must handle extremely well in tight places, have great acceleration. Driver must have good coordination, concentration. Speedway racing is similar to flat tracking, but with specialized lightweight motorcycles.

*Street Chopper*

It is not necessary to run full fairings on road-racing machines, as shown by this full street equipped bike running a number plate taped over the headlight. For any kind of racing, full leather clothing, good boots, gloves, and an approved helmet are imperative.

Although full fairings might be used on a street bike, they are at best advantage on racing bike. Note that these road racers have fairings on seat rear, giant front wheel brakes.

*Street Chopper*

*Cycle Guide*

The drag racing/unstreamlined Bonneville bike is far different from other kinds of racers, stresses pure power. Note stubby handlebars, no front brakes, tiny gas tank built as part of frame top tube. Extremely high top speeds are possible with such a bike, but it is nearly impossible to ride on the street.

*Cycle Guide*

The other extreme from maximum horsepower with big twin engines is tiny displacement "mini-racers." These bikes are usually built from mini-bike components, are used for both drag racing and on Bonneville Salt Flats in Utah, can reach speeds over 100 mph.

*Street Chopper*

Even stock type mini-bikes get a run at the salt flats, where top speeds may not exceed 55 mph. It's all a part of the fun in motorcycling.

This famous Honda speed record attempt was plagued by problems. Fully streamlined bikes like this are going for 300 mph records now and 400 mph should be possible the experts claim. Such bikes are very expensive and only for professional riders.

Harley-Davidson salt flat racer is example of pure horsepower machine in unstreamlined classes. Note lack of fins around cylinders, no cover on primary chain or clutch (saves weight). Rigid frame (no rear suspension) does not hamper drag racing or Bonneville runs.

Look close and you'll see that this dog doesn't mind racing through the desert. Rider tapes pieces of carpet to gas tank. Dog has been enjoying the races since a puppy; both dog and rider are well known competitors in Southern California off-road events.

*Both photos Cycle Guide*

This is what a champion Moto-Cross rider on a Husqvarna bike looks like. The really good riders have total control of the bike whether on or off the ground; sometimes they even set the bike up for a turn while still in the air. All that mud comes from super gooey courses common to most Moto-Cross races.

Note how this frame has been stretched to get extra wheelbase for drag racing. This keeps the front end down (wheelies cost valuable seconds in drag racing). Driver lays low to cut wind resistance.

*All photos Street Chopper*

Harley-Davidson, built for drag racing only, uses fairing, front wheel brakes. Driver sits low and to the rear to aid traction.

Honda 4 drag racer is typical machine, with stubby handlebars, tachometer mounted right in front of rider's face.

*Street Chopper*

Most of the really fast drag bikes have lots of cubic inch displacement (Honda 4 and Harley-Davidson are most popular) and sometimes twin engines are used. Nitromethane fuel is commonly used. Some bikes have over 400 horsepower; speeds are now nearly 200 mph for the quarter-mile.

RIGHT: Tremendously popular with world-wide bike racing fans are the road-racing sidecars. Sidehack rider leans far out on turn to keep bike from tipping, lies flat behind small windshield on straights to cut wind resistance.

If the rear tire breaks loose in drag racing, the elapsed time will go up in dramatic smoke.

*Cycle Guide*

*Street Chopper*

Antique motorcycles are coming into popularity. This twin was built by Sears. Note the bicycle-type pedals used on early motorcycles, for starting and helping the small engines pull steep hills.

Famous Flying Merkel motorcycles had swing action rear suspension, V-twin motors, chain drives.

An early single-cylinder Pierce. Lever just ahead of engine tightens the belt drive to rear wheel; no transmission is used. Note twin-fork front end that looks like modern bicycle forks.

These old-timer photos are of bikes in the Harrah's museum in Reno, Nevada. This Militair had four-cylinder inline engine and transmission like a car, shaft drive to rear wheel. Wheels are wood spoke, "training wheels" and rear end could be lifted after bike was underway.

The Henderson inline four remained after most of other early motorcycles were gone. Company discontinued production before WW II.

scope of this chapter. Don't get down in the dumps. By the time you have gone far enough to perform the basic checks outlined in this chapter, you'll be able to either fix it yourself or give the local mechanic a good idea of what's wrong.

Almost any used bike will benefit from a change of oil. Oil is important to the operation of the engine and the gearbox, and in the case of the two-stroke engine is burned along with the fuel to lubricate the engine. In most two-stroke engines today, the oil is metered to the engine by a small pump. The oil is stored in a small tank usually located under the seat. The service portion of the shop manual will show you what type of oil to run in your bike if it is a two-stroke. Always use the recommended oil. Nothing can ruin a two-stroke engine faster than the wrong oil.

The gearbox or transmission will use a separate oil system. Most bikes should be serviced just like a car, but at more frequent intervals. When you start going over the bike you just bought, a good place to start getting it ready to ride is an oil change. If you have a bike that uses an oil filter (most bikes don't) it should be changed also. When you drain the oil, check it for signs of metal particles or other foreign objects that might suggest problems in the gearbox or lower end.

On many bikes, particularly dirt bikes, the air filter is designed to use a small amount of oil to filter the dust and grit out of the incoming air. If the one on your bike is clogged with dirt, rinse it in a pan of gasoline to get rid of the old oil and dirt, then squeeze it as dry as possible be-fore re-oiling it. The trick way to put a good oil film on the filter element without getting it all over yourself is to take some oil that is designed to mix with gas in a two-stroke engine and add it to a small quantity of gas in a shallow pan. Stir it until it is mixed evenly, then immerse the filter element in it. Squeeze it until it is wet like a sponge, then hang it up to dry on the clothesline. The gas will evaporate, leaving the oil in the filter. It works fine, and is less messy than any other way I know of for oiling a filter element.

An area that shouldn't be overlooked when tuning a used bike is the exhaust. The muffler inside the tailpipe of most bikes is removable, and should be taken out and cleaned. This is most important in the case of the two-stroke. Be-cause the two-stroke burns oil in the gas, it produces a lot more carbon smoke than the four-stroke engine. This car-bon can build up in the tailpipe until it causes a noticeable loss of power, and most guys never think to check the muffler until the bike almost quits.

After you have removed the muffler or baffle from the tailpipe (which can be quite a job in itself if the buildup has frozen it in place), the carbon has to be removed by burning it out. Don't try to soak it out with solvent, it doesn't work. Use a butane or gas welding torch to burn the carbon until it turns to powder, then finish the cleanup with a wire brush.

The clutch, brakes, and throttle are all operated with

cables. These cables require a bit of attention on the used bike; they should be checked for crimps or kinks in the outside housings, and for broken strands showing at the ends. If you are in doubt about the condition of any of the control cables on your bike, change them. It will prevent you from having to worry about the problem when you're thirty miles from nowhere in the middle of the night. The brakes should be adjusted, and if you think they might be worn to the point where they should be replaced or rebuilt, do it now. They are another one of those things that must be working correctly before you try that first ride.

Unless the bike you bought is a complete basket case, there isn't anything too complicated for the average guy to fix in a couple of evenings' work. Who knows! You just may find that you like getting your hands dirty working on your bike. Sometimes the challenge of fixing things that go wrong with a motorcycle turns out to be a new hobby. A couple of guys I know wound up in the motorcycle repair business just because they bought used bikes the first time around!

# The Engine

Motorcycling takes many forms. For some it's getting out in the dirt to go cow-trailing or off-road racing, for others it's a means of getting from one end of the country to the other on two wheels. Some riders limit their use of motorcycles to a tiny two-wheeler used to run between the campsite and the village store, others climb aboard specially designed bikes with nitro-burning engines and rip through the measured quarter mile at speeds of 175 mph, or scream across the Bonneville salt flats at over 250 mph in search of a new land-speed record.

Most of us fall between these two extremes. For many the motorcycle does double duty as both transportation and recreation. But whatever the intention, the motorcycle rider of today has a wonderful and sometimes confusing array of motorcycle engines to choose from, each designed to perform a specific function. There are huge

V-twins, tiny two-strokes that get over fifty miles on a gal-
lon of gas, engines just for street use, and engines whose
sole purpose is to allow the rider to cover the ground in the
shortest amount of time. The beginning rider looking for
a bike can purchase just about any possible type of powerplant he needs for whatever purpose he intends.

All motorcycle engines are broken down into two groups,
the four-stroke engines that function like the one in your
car, and the two-stroke engines that are most popular for
off-road use. Both are internal-combustion engines, both
are air-cooled, but the differences between the two-stroke
and four-stroke principles of operation should be understood before the beginning rider looks for a motorcycle of
his own.

## Four-Stroke Engines

The four-stroke gets it name from the fact that one
complete cycle of operation requires four separate piston movements. It operates just like the automobile engine that we are all familiar with. The first stroke is the
intake stroke. A mixture of gas and air is pulled into the
combustion chamber by the downward movement of
the piston in the cylinder. The intake valve is open at that
point to allow the air/gas mix into the cylinder. As the
piston reaches the bottom of its travel and starts back up,
the intake valve closes, trapping the mix inside. This first
upward movement of the piston is called the compression

51

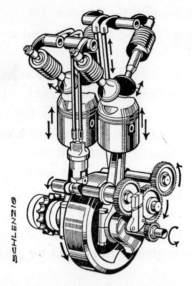

Conventional vertical twin.

stroke. Compression of the air and gas is required to produce the rapid burning (almost an explosion) which
powers the engine. The compressed gas is fired by the
spark plug just as the piston reaches top dead center in
the cylinder, and the powerful force created by the expansion of the burning gases pushes the piston down in the
cylinder to provide the motive force for the bike. This
downward stroke is known as the power stroke.

Just before the piston reaches the bottom of the cylinder
for the second time in the cycle, the exhaust valve opens.
Since the gases are still under some pressure, they will start

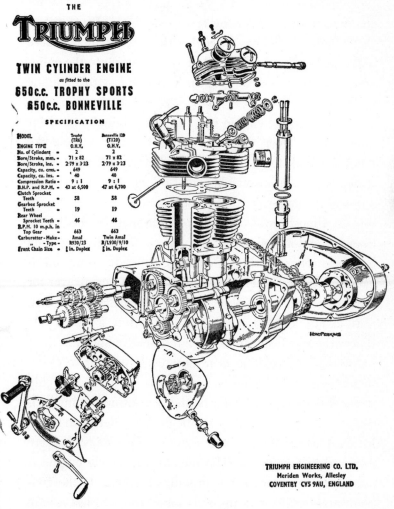

# THE TRIUMPH

## TWIN CYLINDER ENGINE
### as fitted to the
## 650c.c. TROPHY SPORTS
## 650c.c. BONNEVILLE

### SPECIFICATION

| MODEL | Trophy (TR6) | Bonneville 120 (T120) |
|---|---|---|
| ENGINE TYPE | O.H.V. | O.H.V. |
| No. of Cylinders = | 2 | 2 |
| Bore/Stroke, mm. = | 71 x 82 | 71 x 82 |
| Bore/Stroke, ins. = | 2·79 x 3·23 | 2·79 x 3·23 |
| Capacity, cu. cms. = | 649 | 649 |
| Capacity, cu. ins. = | 40 | 40 |
| Compression Ratio = | 9 : 1 | 9 : 1 |
| B.H.P. and R.P.M. = | 43 at 6,500 | 47 at 6,700 |
| Clutch Sprocket Teeth = | 58 | 58 |
| Gearbox Sprocket Teeth = | 19 | 19 |
| Rear Wheel Sprocket Teeth = | 46 | 46 |
| R.P.M. 10 m.p.h. in Top Gear = | 663 | 663 |
| Carburetter - Make = | Amal | Twin Amal |
| " - Type = | R930/23 | R/L930/9/10 |
| Front Chain Size = | ⅜ in. Duplex | ⅜ in. Duplex |

TRIUMPH ENGINEERING CO. LTD.
Meriden Works, Allesley
COVENTRY CV5 9AU, ENGLAND

Cutaway courtesy of Triumph shows 650 Triumph twin with integral transmission.

flowing out of the cylinder. As the piston starts back up for the final time, it forces the rest of the burned fuel out of the cylinder, and when it reaches the top, the intake valve will open to start a new load of air and gas into the cylinder. That, very basically, is the way a four-stroke engine works.

The four-stroke engine was the one originally used for motorcycles. Over the years since the first bicycle-like machines took to the road, a great many different four-stroke engines, some small, some so large they rivaled the automobile engines of their time in power, have been produced. Almost always they have been more sophisticated than the automobile engines of their time, having such things as roller bearings, overhead cams, dry sump lubrication, and the ability to produce far more horsepower for their size than automobile engines. As a matter of fact, until as late as 1960, it was possible to buy a motorcycle that was easily faster than any but all-out racing cars.

Although the engine in a motorcycle is built to closer tolerances, and the parts are smaller and more highly stressed than car engine parts, there is nothing so mysterious about them as to keep the beginning rider from doing his own work. We covered most of the things that are required in Chapter 3. The modern motocycle engine is one of the best engineered products available to the general public today and, properly cared for, will last a long time without expensive repairs.

To illustrate, let's take one of the most popular four-stroke engines on the market today and see how it is constructed. The Honda 750 Four is a top-of-the-line road machine capable of being ridden from coast to coast at freeway speeds without problems. It is also one of the quickest-accelerating bikes built, and is much favored by riders as a starting place for hop-up techniques. Yes, hop-up. There is a booming industry developing for the rider who wants even more power from his bike than it comes with from the factory. Just like a generation of car builders and hotrodders before, the American motorcycle rider soon decides that his personal transportation could use just a bit more pep, even if it's the fastest bike he can buy!

The Honda 750 is actually 736 cc's (such size inflation is common in motorcycling advertising, and many bikes that are called 750, 350, or whatever, are smaller or larger than that). The Honda Four is much like any small four-cylinder engine found in sports cars and some of the recent import economy cars, except that it is turned sideways in the frame. The crankshaft, which runs across the frame, is held in two cast case halves which split into top and bottom parts instead of left and right sides like most other engines. The engine cases also contain the entire transmission, which is connected to the crank by a special chain running back from the center of the crankshaft. The four cylinders are pressed steel liners held in a finned alloy box that bolts on the top of the cases. The cylinder head attaches to the top of the cylinder section and contains the entire cam train in what is called an overhead-cam configuration. By placing the cam as close to the valve as possible, much of the flexing of valve-train components that takes place at high rpm's is avoided, and the engine will continue to produce power at much higher revs than is possible with other layouts.

Each cylinder has a separate carburetor. There are four in all, controlled through a positive cable arrangement by the hand throttle. The clutch, which is mounted on the side of the transmission section of the cases, is a wet unit, which means that it is designed to run in a bath of cooling oil. Oil control is handled as in many expensive race cars. The main supply is not carried inside the engine, but is maintained in a separate tank with a pump and a set of external lines to carry the oil to and from the engine. Exhaust is handled by four separate exhaust pipes, each with it own muffler. The engine puts out over 60 hp at a rated 8,000 rpm and is capable of being turned in excess of 12,000 rpm without failure. All in all, it's quite a potent package.

The Honda engine is capable of accelerating through a measured quarter mile in under 13 seconds and, if state laws would permit, is able to maintain an effortless 100 mph for long distances. We didn't choose the Honda Four because it is an outstanding example of the new breed of high-horsepower motorcycles, but because it has all the features found in many other engines that are capable of giving similar performance. With only a couple of exceptions, the entire group of large, fast motorcycles available in this country are able to give the rider all the performance he wants just as they come from the dealer.

For the more economy-minded, there are smaller engines made by all the manufacturers that will fill just about any need. For limited off-road use almost any four-stroke engine of 350 cc's or less will do well. It's not until the rider tries to use the bike in competitive events such as motocross that the four-stroke loses some of its effectiveness. For simple cow-trailing or play racing, the four-stroke is more than ready to take the rider any place he wants to go. Because it is silent and smooth-running compared to the two-stroke engine, the four-stroke is a good bet in smaller sizes for around-town running, or as a moneysaver in getting to and from school.

If you want to increase the power of your bike as you become more proficient at riding, you will find that the four-stroke motorcycle engine responds to the same hop-up treatments as the automobile engine. Increased displacement is the fastest way to more power, and many companies offer "big bore" kits to make the job of enlarging the size of the engine easier. Usually these kits consist of the new, larger cylinders or liners (some require that the old cylinder be sent in for machine work), the larger pistons, plus all the small parts such as gaskets which will be required to finish the job. Many companies also include some basic tuning information to help the mechanic get everything going after the installation is done.

Other hop-up items that work well are modified exhausts (check local noise laws before purchasing), racing cams, more efficient carburetion, and on many engines, high-compression racing heads to add to the horsepower. Once the rider has learned how to handle the bike with stock horsepower, he can go just about as far as he wants to increase the power of his engine.

Along with high-performance engine items, there are a host of things that will improve handling and braking so that the bike will be perfectly safe to ride with increased power. In short, the sky is the limit for the motorcycle rider who wants performance, and even the smallest four-stroke engine can be hopped-up to far more than its normal output.

## Two-Stroke Engines

The two-stroke engine is a different concept in internal combustion engines. Unlike the four-stroke, which requires two complete revolutions of the crankshaft to produce the single stroke of power, the two-stroke gets a power stroke each time the piston moves downward in the cylinder. Let's follow a two-stroke engine through one cycle of operation to find out how this is done.

The two-stroke engine has no cam or valves. Intake and exhaust are controlled by a series of openings in the cylinder wall which are covered and uncovered by the piston as it moves up and down. This type of two-stroke engine is known as the Piston-Port engine and is the most common.

To start, imagine that the two-stroke engine is already running and the piston is moving upward in the cylinder to compress an air-gas mixture that has already entered the engine. As the piston moves up, a port in the side of the cylinder is uncovered. This is the intake port, which leads not to the combustion chamber, as you might expect, but allows the incoming air-gas mix into the inside of the engine crankcase. When the piston reaches the top of its travel, the spark plug fires the compressed mixture that was placed in the combustion chamber during the previous cycle. This forces the piston down just as it would in a four-stroke engine. At this point the intake port is blocked by the piston and the mixture in the crankcase is being compressed by the downward movement of the piston. This precompression is necessary to provide some means of pushing the mixture into the combustion chamber at the proper time.

As the piston gets to a certain point on its downward stroke, it uncovers the exhaust port and lets the burned gases out of the cylinder. A little farther down in the cylinder is another opening called the transfer port. When the transfer port is opened by the piston, it allows the com-

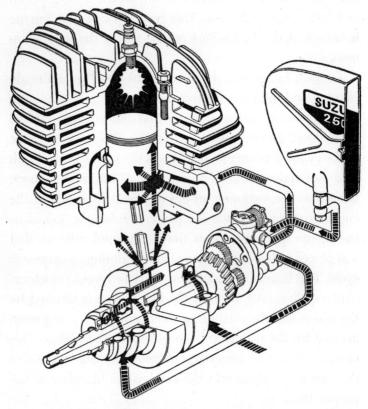

Two-stroke oiling may be by mixing oil with gasoline, or by the more complicated pressure system as used by Suzuki. The latter is better and reduces chances of piston seizure caused by overheating and poor cylinder oiling.

pressed mixture in the crankcase to push its way into the combustion chamber. Because the mixture is under pressure the combustion chamber fills rapidly.

As the piston reaches the bottom of its stroke and starts back up, both the transfer port and exhaust port are blocked and the mixture in the combustion chamber is compressed for firing. At the same time this is taking place, the rising piston has uncovered the intake port again to allow a fresh charge of air and gas to enter the crankcase.

Because the two-stroke produces a stroke of power on each revolution, twice as often as the four-stroke, it is a much more efficient engine under controlled conditions. Its main advantages over the four-stroke are simplicity (no valve train or cams mean fewer moving parts), and the ability to produce more horsepower than a four-stroke of equal size. For these reasons the two-stroke engine dominates many forms of motorcycle competition. Its drawbacks are that the two-stroke generally produces its power in a narrower rpm band than the four-stroke, and must burn a mixture of oil and gas which causes the engine to carbon up at frequent intervals, requiring routine maintenance. The reason for mixing oil with the gas is that the fuel first passes through the crankcases and lack of some lubrication in the fuel would soon cause damage to bearings and piston rings.

Engine construction, except for the absence of the valves and cam, is much the same for the two-stroke as the four-stroke, so we need not go into it in great detail. The only major difference is an oil-mixing pump on most modern two-stroke engines which automatically insures that the correct amount of lubricating oil will be included with the gas. Although the two-stroke has in recent years been produced in a number of large-displacement versions for street use, it is in off-road activities that it really shines. Because it produces so much power for the weight, the two-stroke family of engines has dominated motocross and desert racing for the last few years. Engines like the Swedish Husqvarna and the German Maico, to name just a couple, are nearly unbeatable in off-road activities. Their light weight compared to four-stroke bikes and their sheer ruggedness make them the favorite as soon as the terrain turns to soft dirt.

It is in dirt riding that the most wear and tear occurs in motorcycle engines of all kinds. The most obvious problem is proper air filtration. Unless care is taken to make sure that dust and grit are kept out of the engine, serious damage can be done in a matter of minutes. If you intend to use your bike for serious off-road riding or racing, there are several replacement air filters for the engine that will prevent this problem from causing you worry. Just check with your shop; they'll be glad to help you select the proper element for your bike.

One of the first things that happens to the two-stroke rider is to meet another rider on the same kind of bike and challenge him to a race. To his susprise the other rider disappears in a very short time, his bike being much faster, even though it looks the same. Is it sheer skill that makes the other rider win the race? Probably not. The hop-up market for the two-stroke engine is as big as that for the four-stroke, and a great many off-road riders find that a little extra power turns their showroom kitten into a tiger.

There are several ways to increase the power output of the two-stroke engine, one of the most popular being the replacement of the exhaust pipe with a competition unit known as an expansion chamber. The expansion chamber is a tuned exhaust that has a larger-diameter section in the center. Without going into the engineering of the chamber (which is so complicated that even the engineers don't agree how it works) let's just say it allows the exhaust to leave the engine in such a manner that a considerable amount of horsepower is felt. The expansion chamber changes the operating potential of the engine, causing the rpm band in which the engine makes its useful power to be narrower. This can take a little getting used to. Also some minor rejetting of the carburetion and sometimes a change of spark-plug heat ranges is required. One important thing, check local laws regarding noise before you put on the chamber. It makes the engine much louder and can bring on a confrontation with the police if used in the wrong place.

If you are riding your bike in the country, especially in national forest land or state parks, the expansion chamber may be illegal without some form of spark arrestor. The spark arrestor is required in many places, and you should always be prepared to install one on your bike if the area is one that is restricted. A couple of companies make an approved unit that will fit the end of most expansion chambers. Check the shop where you bought your bike.

Along with the expansion chamber, a number of hop-up items are available at most shops that specialize in off-road riding. High-compression heads, modified pistons, special carburetion, and just about everything you need to turn your bike into a racer are available. In some cases the factory itself has a list of high-performance components that can be ordered to fit your bike. For example, Yamaha has packages of hop-up parts called "GYT KITS" that will raise the performance potential of any of their off-road bikes by quite a bit. Getting the information on what is needed for your bike is simple; just get friendly with the service and parts people who handle your type of bike. They are usually riders and racers themselves, and will be more than willing to show you the correct way to go. They may even have some tips on setting up chassis and suspension for better handling so that you can make full use of all that new power.

It's quite a sensation when you twist the throttle and go charging up a hill that you never could climb before. That extra horsepower pays for itself in sheer fun.

## Working on Your Engine

I've made continued reference to the manual for any kind of engine repair. The reason is simply that the great variety in motorcycle engines and transmissions makes it practically impossible to lump them all into one category. Even so, it is possible to consider each particular power-stroke design, either two- or four-stroke, and take a look at exactly what kind of repair procedure would be expected.

The most common repair to any motorcycle is that of the "top end," or combustion-chamber area. Until the last fifteen years, pulling the cylinder head to scrape the carbon from combustion-chamber surfaces was considered an integral part of owning a motorcycle. The procedure is still applicable to some engines, but great improvements in combustion-chamber efficiency have nearly eliminated the problem. Whether or not your particular engine will need the service periodically is irrelevant here. By removing the head you can get an excellent idea of engine condition and perhaps forestall an early failure.

Don't tear the engine apart until you have the necessary gaskets for reassembly. Ride your machine to the local bike shop and let the parts man give you exactly the pieces you need. Most shops now have special gasket kits for various phases of engine and transmission overhaul. While you're at the bike shop, get a cleaning bucket and solvent, a good stiff parts cleaning brush, and some Gunk. This is an engine-cleaning compound that works wonders on the exterior of motorcycle engines. Clean the entire bike before you start engine disassembly.

Always remove the spark plug before you unbolt the head, as it isn't uncommon for the wrench to slip and waste the plug. Just a little thing, but pennies you save can be applied elsewhere. After all the headbolts are out (some engines use capscrews, others use studs and nuts), tap the head gently if it seems stuck. Never, never force it with a big hammer! And do not pry it with a bar or screwdriver, as this will either mar the combustion chamber, bend a valve, or break a cooling fin. Just be patient.

If the carburetor manifold happens to bolt to the head, remove the manifold/carburetor assembly. It is not necessary to remove the camshaft or rocker-arm assemblies. Any auto-parts store will have a special wire brush for a drill motor to remove carbon buildup. Do not use a screwdriver or chisel to remove the carbon. Rotate the engine until the piston is on top dead center, then remove the carbon from that unit. Be careful to get small pieces of carbon from around the edge of the piston (between the piston top edge and the top piston ring). Make sure there are no pieces of carbon on either head or piston before reassembly.

If the engine has quite a few miles on it, a good valve job may be necessary (four-stroke engine only). Now is the time. You can do your own valve work, but the cost is so low it is really advisable to farm this out to the bike shop. They will check the valves and replace them if necessary. At the same time, they'll be inspecting the valve guides for excessive wear. Of course, if the valves need only be "lapped in," you can do this at home with a couple of inexpensive tools from the auto-parts store.

To lap the valves, you'll need a small stick with a suction-cup end and some valve-lapping compound. Remove the valve springs, put compound on the valve seats, press the suction cup to the valve head and spin the stick between your hands. This is only a tune-up operation, and is not as common now as it once was. If the valves are marginal, always get a full valve job and save headaches later.

Inspect the cylinder area while the head is off. If there is excessive piston-ring wear, there will be a small ridge at the top of the cylinder bore. If this is pronounced, or enough so you can hang a fingernail easily, chances are good you will want to do some cylinder work.

Most cylinders unbolt at the case, which makes the motorcycle engine immediately different from the car engine. Remove the cylinder and take it to the bike shop. If the bore is too far gone, you can either have it bored larger (costly, because that usually means a bigger piston also), or get a new cylinder. If you're thinking about adding a displacement-increasing hop-up kit, this is the time to do it.

If you're sticking with the stock piston, inspect it closely for signs of unusual wear. This will show as long vertical gouges in the piston body, chipped edges around the piston-ring grooves, or discoloration. If any of these signs show, remove the piston and have the bike shop look it over. They will also want to check the piston size with a micrometer. Sometimes when a motorcycle engine gets too hot, the excessive temperature will cause the piston to "collapse," that is, the diameter will shrink slightly. This usually calls for a new piston. New piston rings should always be installed if the cylinder(s) is removed during an overhaul, unless there is very low mileage on the engine.

About the only thing remaining is the bottom end, and this would be the final effort. Of concern will be the oiling system, which may be wet- or dry-sump, and the bearings. A dry-sump oil system merely means the oil is stored in an external tank, while the wet-sump stores all the oil used within the engine case (like most car engines). Inspect the oil-pump gear(s) for any signs of wear, as well as any plates that come in contact with the gears.

It is most difficult to tell the condition of bearings without actually breaking the engine case apart. For the most part, unless the bearings are really shot, the only way to discover excess play is by feel. Place the thumb and forefinger around the rod big end and move the crankshaft slightly. Only the tiniest bit of play should be felt. Feel the crank where it exits the case in the same way.

Both insert and roller bearings are used in motorcycle engines, depending entirely upon the type of crankshaft construction. If the crank is of the "built-up" variety, roller or needle bearings can be expected. This type of crankshaft, which will have the halves bolted or pressed together, is best left to the professional to repair or service.

The bottom end usually doesn't give much trouble unless the bike has been given a hard life.

You follow essentially the same procedure when working with either two- or four-stroke engines, the difference being in valve mechanism. Unless the four-stroke is to get hop-up cams, they will normally not need replacement. Check them anyway, and any lobe that looks different from the others may be flat and need substitution. The big thing to look for at the cam is a worn lobe or scored surface, which tells that future failure is sure.

Make sure the various engine parts are absolutely clean before reassembly. Just before the parts are put together, it eases things if they are coated with assembly lubricant, which may be a special lube from the bike shop, or just plain engine oil. Use something.

Definitely torque all bolts to exactly the specifications called for in the manual, and retorque all bolts after so many miles' or hours' running time, also dictated by the manual.

The two major engine accessories, ignition and carburetion, are almost always a matter of professional setup the first time around. While the shop manual will tell you exactly what the various settings should be, you'll find it money will spent to let a pro do the job first time, with you looking over his shoulder. Mostly, both items are precision units and the secret is in getting the necessary clearances near-perfect.

The engine in your bike is a precision unit that can be

tuned and changed in a variety of ways. Once you get familiar with it, you'll find enjoyment in working to improve the power or just providing routine maintenance. In any case, it's the heart of your bike; get to know it better.

---

# Tuning

The word tuning as applied to things mechanical has come to mean "tune-up," but this isn't the full intent of the word, especially as it applies to motorcycles. While you might be tuning your engine during a tune-up, the word really means everything you do to the vehicle, chassis as well as engine, to get maximum performance in some desired area. With this as a frame of reference, tuning for the bike owner comes to mean making the vehicle run better, stop better, handle better; to make it superior to, or at least equal to, a stock motorcycle. Chassis tuning is normally restricted to the competition bike, however, and is something so personal that only after you become a serious competition rider will you even consider this phase of the work. An engine tune-up implies getting the engine back to some previous level of performance, while performance tuning means improving, or hopping-up, the engine. You even have sub-areas, such as intake ram tuning and exhaust tuning. In this chapter we'll be concerned primarily with returning the engine to some previous state of performance, with an occasional reference to performance tuning. When you feel ready to get into power tuning, turn to your local bike shop for advice, and read all the motorcycle magazines you can find.

## Trouble-Shooting

Doing any kind of tune-up work on either a two- or four-stroke motorcycle engine is easy, and requires very little in the way of tools. It is trying to diagnose the problem that is usually difficult for the amateur mechanic. If three things are all going on in correct sequence and proportion—ignition, fuel, and timing—any internal-combustion engine should run. When you learn to limit your investigation to these three areas, and to thoroughly search out possible problems in each area, you will become something of an expert tuner.

If the engine just dies for no apparent reason, you can first expect the most obvious things; either you ran out of gas, or the switch has been turned off. Seems a rudimentary assumption, but many times this is the extent of a problem. But suppose you have gas in the tank and the ignition key is on, then what? You can still be out of gas or without an operable ignition circuit, by having something wrong in the delivery systems. This makes it easy:

just check to see if you're getting gas at the carburetor, or fire at the spark plug. You can see that trouble-shooting is a matter of starting with the most obvious possibility and working throughout a system until the trouble is found and remedied.

Experience shows that the majority of problems that require trouble-shooting are connected with the electrical system. When a bike quits for no apparent reason, or doesn't start or run well, check for a dead battery or an ignition failure at the condenser, a loose ground wire, or burned points. At the same time, inspect for low battery water, a bad generator or regulator (a bad regulator will cause the battery to run low on water rapidly). Since the battery is usually behind the engine and away from fresh air, always check constantly to make sure the water level is up.

Wiring is not usually a problem causer, although very old wiring should be replaced if it is cracked or the insulation is worn through. Keep wiring well away from a sharp metal edge where it can eventually wear through and short out.

The preliminary inspection then shifts to the fuel system, where the culprit is almost invariably contaminated gasoline. While a broken carburetor part or a fuel line failure can occur, the majority of problems are caused by water or some other foreign object in the gas.

Water is a common occurence in motorcycle gas tanks, and it usually comes from the bottom of a service station storage tank. Never discount water as the reason for an engine suddenly stopping or refusing to start. It is also possible to pick up other types of foreign material, such as rust scale or dirt, usually from a gas can from the home garage. When water is involved, the engine will often continue to run, but it will be erratic and tend to sputter. The exhaust may even turn the pipe blue because of a lean running condition.

Water is heavier than gasoline and settles to the tank bottom. Lean the bike to the outlet tap side, remove the carburetor bowl and look for water (it may be obvious, or it may be only little beads adhering to the bowl sides and bottom). Take off the fuel line at the carburetor and allow the water to run away (do not shake up the fuel and water before draining) until pure gas is flowing. Wipe the carburetor dry, and the engine should run. To get rid of any remaining small amount of water, mix a small cup of wood alcohol with the gas, which will absorb the water and burn in the combustion chamber.

If there is uncontaminated fuel getting to the carburetor, the trouble may be inside the carb. Amal-type side valve carburetors have ticklers that function as a choke, while the butterfly designs rely on a closed butterfly to draw in raw fuel for starting. With the mixture richened, crank the engine over a few times with the throttle open and the switch off. This will pull the mixture into the combustion chamber—if there is a mixture. Now open the throttle slightly, just enough to get some air into the intake manifolding, and advance the spark if manually controlled (one-half advance). If the engine has a release for compression, turn the engine until the piston starts down after top dead center on the compression stroke. Now kick the engine over briskly without opening the throttle the minute it catches (same procedure with electric start). The engine should spin through easily, and even with poor mixture or other fuel problems, or weak coil or poor points, the engine will run. If the engine still won't run, the trouble-shooting gets serious.

Start at the ignition switch, because the switch can be bad or the mag kill button can be grounded. Move the key around a little, try the lights and horn, anything to make sure there is electricity getting from the battery to the engine (the battery cable can be corroded, remember). Check the lead to the coil by removing the hot wire and tapping it against metal. If there is no electricity to the coil, suspect bad connections on either the hot or ground side of the battery. If fuses are in the system, inspect them very carefully. If in doubt, install a spare. (Use a piece of chewing-gum foil wrapped around the fuse only as an emergency, and replace as soon as possible. If wiring starts to smoke with the emergency fuse short cut, turn everything off, because you've got a direct ground somewhere.)

If you still have no electrical power, the battery must be the cause. Check by shorting momentarily between the battery terminals with a pair of pliers. There should be a good, sharp crackle when the poles are touched, enough to burn the plier handle ends slightly. A good battery will crackle, a weak battery will just sizzle, or do nothing. Sometimes, when an electric starter is used, a kind of clicking sizzle will come from the battery. This is from a poor connection. A poor connection will prevent a battery from charging correctly.

It is possible for the engine to run with a poor battery, but you might get some symptoms that lead you to suspect other problems, like point float or carburetion. Tighten all the battery leads, and turn them slightly in the process to ensure good connections.

The next area to investigate is the spark plug. Most plugs will work, after a fashion, even though they are burned badly. If the plug tip is wet with gas or oil, or has a piece of carbon stuck between the electrodes, it is fouled and may not run even after a good cleaning and adjustment. This is particularly true of two-stroke plugs. Sometimes the combination of a weak spark from the ignition and a slightly fouled plug team to keep the engine from running. Close the plug gap slightly if a weak spark is involved. Check spark by connecting the plug wire, grounding the plug metal base against the engine and turning the engine over briskly. If the spark is reddish, it is weak. A weak, reddish flame at the spark plug indicates the condenser is bad. A healthy spark will be brisk and bright blue/white. This test will also reveal a bad plug. If you're getting fire to the plug, but not across the gap, the plug is grounded internally. If you are getting fire at the magneto/distributor, but not at the plug end of the plug wire, replace the wire. Sometimes secondary wire can look perfect and be broken inside.

Next check the ignition. Remove the cover and rotate the engine until the distributor cam is on the low side, with the point follower on the cam heel. Turn the key on and snap the points apart. If they do not spark, the trouble can be a bad condenser, dirty or burned points, or a ground in the point wiring.

Check the coil. Remove the secondary lead between coil and ignition and ground it to the engine or frame. If there is no spark (key on), the coil is probably bad. But check the coil wire lead, as it can be bad. Fire to the ignition but not to the points indicates a short in the point wiring, usually at an insulation point. Also look for a broken wire. Ground across the point wth a screwdriver, and if you get a spark this way, the point tips are bad. Points seem to have a short lifespan in motorcycles, so expect to replace them often.

Make sure the points are actually opening by turning the engine until the point follower is on the apex of the distributor cam. If the points close even a slight amount, the engine will start to misfire under load and at high rpm, and if the points finally close the engine won't start at all. If you don't have a feeler gauge handy, something about the thickness of a cigarette paper is close.

Magneto problems are generally related to points, coil failure, bad condenser, kill-button wire disconnected or grounded, or point gap too wide or closed.

If you have strong fire at the plug, check to see that the

engine is in time. Sometimes a mechanical part can break or get out of kilter in the ignition drive system and the timing will be thrown completely off. The plug should fire at about the time the piston is at top dead center on compression stroke.

If you still have a problem, turn again to the fuel system.

Start by checking for a plugged vent in the tank. If the engine will start, but then stops, this can be the cause. Remove the tank cap and if the engine keeps running, or starts for the first time, clean the cap vent or get a new cap. Rust and dirt can build up around the carburetor screen and choke off gas. If gas is getting to the carburetor, but the spark-plug tip is dry, chances are the carburetor is not choking correctly. Place the hand over the carb inlet as the engine is turned over to pull gas into the engine. Be careful here or you'll flood the engine with too much gas.

Check the bowl to see if the needle valve is stuck closed by rust or dirt, which will cause the bowl to be dry. If there is any doubt about the carburetor condition, or you've just bought a used bike and you're trying to make it run, rebuild the carburetor. If the engine kicks back when starting, there is too much ignition advance. A manual advance is easy to adjust, an automatic advance might be inoperative. Should the air filter get clogged, the engine will run progressively richer, and if the muffler is clogged the engine will be hard to start.

If an engine stops or staggers when the throttle is opened quickly (a slight stagger is not uncommon), the

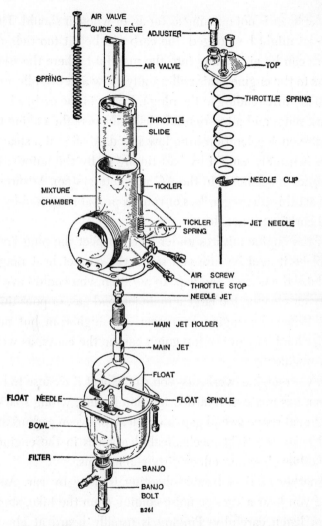

AIR VALVE
GUIDE SLEEVE
ADJUSTER
AIR VALVE
SPRING
TOP
THROTTLE SPRING
THROTTLE SLIDE
NEEDLE CLIP
MIXTURE CHAMBER
TICKLER
TICKLER SPRING
JET NEEDLE
AIR SCREW
THROTTLE STOP
NEEDLE JET
MAIN JET HOLDER
MAIN JET
FLOAT
FLOAT NEEDLE
FLOAT SPINDLE
BOWL
FILTER
BANJO
BANJO BOLT
B261

Exploded view of an Amal carburetor. Key to keeping these carbs fit is straight jet needle of correct size, smooth throttle-slide/valve action.

choke lever is not opening as far as, or when, it should. The idle jet might be clogged, the carb can be set too rich, or there can be air leaking into the manifold where the carb bolts to the engine (this will usually show as a fast idle and lean mixture reading at the plug). Water in the carb, a bad spark plug, and a too rich idle will all cause the engine to misfire on acceleration from low speed. Misfire at a steady rpm is usually caused by bad timing or by the automatic advance mechanism in the AC magneto system. Misfiring at a set throttle, regardless of rpm, is probably caused by a bad carburetor needle.

If the engine misfires under load, suspect the plug first. Replace it, and be sure you select the correct heat range and use the correct end gap. In addition, you could have a dirty air cleaner, too large a main jet, bad gas, or poor timing. When the engine runs poorly at high rpm but not under load, any of the foregoing can be the cause, as well as valve float.

If your engine overheats, you can expect the cause to be a lean gas mixture, retarded ignition timing, wrong sparkplug heat range or end gap, an air leak between carburetor and head, too tight mechanical clearances in the engine, low oil level, wrong oil, or dirty cooling fins.

Another kind of trouble-shooting is done by ear. Any time you hear a strange noise coming from the bike, stop. Then listen carefully. Pinging is usually heard at about half-speed and is louder during acceleration. It is caused by pre-ignition in the combustion chamber. You're using too low an octane gasoline, or the ignition is advanced too far. An excess of carbon buildup in the combustion chamber can cause a glowing hot spot which will set off the incoming mixture before the plug does, and this kind of pre-ignition will often burn a hole in the piston. Don't let the engine keep running when you hear a strange noise, because piston seizure is right around the corner.

A screech or whine from the engine is often caused by roller bearings going bad, while a knock on acceleration might mean bad shell-type bearings. A double knock, like a kind of click-clack at idle, indicates a bad piston pin. Piston slap common to the air-cooled engine should not be confused with this noise. Clatter is usually more of a staccato sound, and comes from the valve mechanism. A high-pitched whirring or singing noise can be caused by a bad timing gear.

There is one last little thing to check in the trouble-shooting sequence, and it would probably be done when the spark plug is being checked. Unless the mixture is compressed sufficiently, it is possible the engine will run poorly, or won't even start. That means you must check compression. Put your finger over the open spark-plug hole and turn the engine over. If your finger is pushed off the plug hole, you have compression. If you can hold your finger in place during the compression stroke, you've got internal mechanical problems (hole in piston, broken rings, and so on). The engine should not be run until these problems are fixed.

## Trouble-Shooting Guide

ENGINE WON'T START

1. Gas tank empty.
2. Tank valve closed.
3. Gas line clogged.
4. Battery discharged; poor connections.
5. Fouled spark plugs.
6. Plug cables broken or leaking.
7. Ignition points closed.
8. Ignition points misaligned.
9. Loose wiring in battery-ignition circuit.
10. Bad coil.
11. Bad condenser.
12. Hanging valves.
13. Engine flooded.

ENGINE STARTS HARD

1. Plugs bad or partially fouled.
2. Plug cables broken or leaking.
3. Ignition points nearly closed or misaligned.
4. Battery low on charge.
5. Loose wire in battery-ignition circuit.
6. Bad coil.
7. Bad condenser.
8. Carburetor out of adjustment.
9. Spark timing incorrect.

ENGINE RUNS ERRATICALLY OR MISFIRES

1. Plugs bad or partially fouled.
2. Plug cables broken or leaking.

3. Plug end gap incorrect (too wide or too narrow).
4. Points misaligned or dirty.
5. Bad coil.
6. Bad condenser.
7. Condenser wiring loose.
8. Battery charge low.
9. Loose wire in battery-ignition circuit.
10. Damaged wiring shorting intermittently.
11. Water or other foreign matter in fuel.
12. Gas-tank vent clogged.
13. Carburetor out of adjustment.
14. Valve springs weak or broken.

## CARBURETOR FLOODS

1. Float level too high.
2. Needle valve sticking or seat or needle worn excessively.
3. Foreign material at needle-valve seat.
4. Float binding in bowl.

## SPARK PLUGS FOUL

1. Plug range too cold.
2. Bad rings.
3. Excessive valve-guide wear.

## PRE-IGNITION

1. Carbon buildup in combustion chamber or on piston.
2. Plug range too hot.
3. Bad Plugs.
4. Ignition timing advanced too far.

DETONATION

1. Gas octane too low.
2. Excessive carbon buildup in combustion chamber.

OVERHEATING

1. Poor oil supply, poor circulation.
2. Leaking valves.
3. Gas/air mixture too lean.
4. Ignition timing late.


## Tuning

Now that the diagnosis of a poor running engine is completed, and hopefully the offending area has been isolated and cured, a general tune-up can be considered. Essentially, this is nothing more than bringing the engine up to some prescribed standard, be it the factory-recommended settings, or other criteria established by the rider from experience.

To begin with, don't tinker with the engine because there is nothing else to do. More poorly running motorcycles can be attributed to an overzealous owner than to mechanical malfunction. A serious, and successful, tuner goes about his job methodically. When tuning the four-stroke, for example, he will consider valve timing, spark timing, valve clearances, fuel/air ratio, and point/plug gapping. All these areas must be coordinated to get the best results.

To start with, set the valve lash at exactly what the manufacturer specifies, using a dial indicator if available, a feeler gauge otherwise. After the engine has been run for a while, check and reset the clearances if necessary. Valve timing is directly affected by the valve-to-rocker clearance, a slight variation here being the same as running a modified camshaft.

The point gap should be set as nearly perfect as possible, using a round feeler gauge. If the points are pitted, install new ones, and make sure the two points are aligned. Set the ignition timing, start the engine, and check the automatic advance with a timing light. Timing off either way, advanced or retarded, will have an effect on how the engine starts and runs.

Make sure you have a spark plug with the correct heat range and set the gap to what the manufacturer recommends. Then install it with a torque wrench. Warm the engine and set the idle to give a moderately fast idle speed. Run the slow-speed adjusting screw in until the engine starts to stumble, then back it out one-quarter turn. Turn the throttle crisply; if the engine stumbles, richen the mixture slightly until it takes the throttle well. Readjust the idle mixture to give the idle speed you like.

Blueprinting a four-stroke engine is a form of fine tuning that is essentially making sure the mechanical apparatus is exactly as the factory specifications specify. It is a form of performance tune-up, but not necessarily hopping-up.

A production engine will be built close to engineering

specifications, but it will not be perfect. For this reason, the actual power output and the designed output are different. To begin any blueprinting job, you must start with the factory engineering specs. Usually these are available direct from the factory. If the engine is multi-cylinder, each part of each cylinder must be identical in every way.

Machining tolerances vary considerably with every engine, so the combustion chamber is the place to start with blueprinting. To find out what the real compression ratio is, turn the engine so the spark-plug hole is vertical and the piston is at top dead center on the compression stroke. Use a chemical beaker graduated in cubic centimeters (cc's) and pour either water or a mixture of paraffin and thin oil into the chamber until the fluid is at the bottom edge of the spark-plug-hole threads. Note the exact amount of fluid the chamber accepted. You get the compression ratio by using this equation:

$$\frac{\text{engine cc's} + \text{fluid volume in chamber}}{\text{fluid volume in chamber}} = \text{compression ratio}$$

The chamber volume will usually be less than factory recommendation, and can be modified either by filing the head (not easy) or using slightly higher-compression pistons.

On a multi-cylinder engine, remove the head(s) and pour each chamber full of fluid. Open up all chambers to match the chamber holding the greatest amount of fluid. Use that amount in the foregoing equation, and then select a higher-compression piston to suit. If you don't know what piston to use, just tell the piston manufacturer what compression you really have, and he'll take it from there. The head(s) can be milled slightly to raise the compression, also.

Check all internal clearances, such as main and rod bearings, and adjust them, as they will have an effect on performance, especially if they are too tight. Check the cylinder bore, and the piston-to-cylinder wall clearances, and hone if necessary to get the correct clearance. Definitely check the piston-ring end gap and land-side clearance.

Use a dial indicator on the valve stem to determine exactly what the camshaft timing is. Remember that a slight change in rocker/stem clearance will have an effect on valve timing, and all cylinders should have the same thing. Set this timing at what the factory calls for. Later you'll learn how to open or close the clearance slightly to increase either bottom- or top-end power. Finally, check the ignition timing to make sure the points are opening at exactly the place they are supposed to relative to piston position in the cylinder. You'll need a degree wheel for this (a wheel marked in 360 degrees) attached to the crankshaft. It is inexpensive and available at most bike shops or automotive speed shops.

The procedures outlined above are for the four-stroke engine, but they apply equally to the two-stroke, although there will be no valves involved with the latter. The two-stroke will be very definitely affected by ignition timing, which must be as near perfect as possible, and the spark plug must be in excellent condition. If there is any doubt about the plug, get a new one.

A final reminder on both types of bike: make sure the carburetor float is set at the correct height. If it is off, and it can get off through ordinary use, the engine may not run smoothly at any rpm. This should be one of the first things you check during a tune-up.

Tuning a motorcycle engine is not difficult, and it does not take a lot of time. But you do not want to overlook a single item on the list, and you never want to "take a chance" with a part that is doubtful. Parts are usually inexpensive, and this is the only way to assure maximum performance all the time. Only then will riding be as pleasureful as it should be.

# 6

# Transmissions, Sprockets, and Chains

Way back in the 1800s when the automobile was being invented, a chain was used to drive the rear wheels. That same kind of final drive was used on cars well into the twentieth century, and it remains the favorite type of power-trasmission device for motorcycles today. There are notable exceptions to chain drive, the German BMW shaft drive being the most famous, but the chain system is so low-cost and maintenance-free it is likely to remain on motorcycles for years to come.

Fortunately, motorcycle final drive is not nearly as complicated as that for an automobile. But it does require a knowledge of chain repair, and at least a casual understanding of transmission/clutch operation. Since the motorcycle drive units are quite small, they can generally be repaired at home with a manual as guide, and parts are inexpensive. However, it is always wise to get parts orders in right away, since the dealer might have to order from a regional warehouse, or even from the factory.

The number-one mistake a new bike owner makes is disassembling his motorcycle without regard to how things come apart. While it is absolutely essential for every owner to have a good manual as part of his equipment, it is also true that some manuals do not give the kind of exploded-view analysis of a system that the amateur mechanic needs. When something like a clutch assembly or transmission is being worked on, it should be removed from the bike and set aside where all the parts can be laid out in order of disassembly. If things get confusing, use a piece of masking tape to number the parts in consecutive order. Do *not* tear the thing apart and toss all the pieces in a box! If you haul this box full of chaos in to the local dealer for reassembly, chances are good it will cost upwards of twice as much as the original repair might have.

Before getting into the basics of final-drive maintenance, we should look more closely at what makes up the motorcycle transmission system. A transmission is necessary because an internal-combustion engine as we know it has a very limited power range and therefore must use leverage multiplication to move the bike from a standstill. While the average production road bike will have up to five speeds in the gearbox, some racing bikes have six speeds, and some really exotic racing motorcycles have used as many as twelve speeds.

Two different-size gears running together are really just

a form of leverage, the same as a long plank and a fulcrum. If the typical road motorcycle has a low gear with 3:1 reduction, this simply means the engine torque from the crankshaft is multiplied three times. Since the typical motorcycle also has a variety of gears and sprockets between the crankshaft and the rear wheel, an almost infinite variety of gearing is possible. The reason most motorcycles, especially those with high-revving engines, use four or five gears is to keep vehicle speed compatible with the engine power band. For instance, one of the wild road-racing bikes may have an engine that produces most power between 8,000 and 10,000 rpm. On a hill or curve where the engine might lug below 8,000, power will drop off drastically. If only three speeds are in the gearbox, the engine might rev over the red-line of, say, 10,500 rpm if low gear is used. Slip in another intermediate gear and the engine can be kept at its best power range. As a rule, motorcycle designers like to keep the spacing between any two ratios no greater than 12 percent. Fortunately, the motorcycle engine is not giving out the gobs of torque and horsepower common to the larger automobile engines, so the transmission/clutch assembly is not large.

Along with the vast improvement in motorcycle-engine design has come a similar upgrading of the clutch, yet the basic design remains quite unchanged from that of several decades ago. Essentially, the improvements have been to make the clutch capable of handling much larger torque loads while simplifying the construction details. The majority of clutch systems in use today are of the "stacked disc" design, which is a departure from the automotive-type clutch. The motorcycle clutch is different in that the input and output shaft must be on the same side of the unit, rather than opposite ends as with a car. This means that some form of housing will be employed which will be connected either to the engine or the transmission (usually the latter), the housing either used to drive the transmission gears or to accept the engine torque (the housing is thus either driven or driving, according to design). The housing will have slots in the perimeter which accept tabs on the outer edge of clutch disc plates, discs which in turn will have large holes in the center. A shaft coming through the housing will have similar clutch discs that attach only to the shaft. When the clutch is free, the center shaft and the housing will not turn together because the two sets of clutch plates are not touching. Springs are fixed to an outside plate which covers the clutch discs so that strong spring pressure will hold the discs in contact. When the clutch lever is actuated, this spring-loaded plate is pulled away from the discs and the clutch is free. Usually, clutch systems are not this simple, but they all work on this basic principle.

Before you ever start work on a clutch, suspect the problem as possibly being in the clutch cable adjustment. If the cable to too "tight," the clutch springs are not released completely so the discs will tend to slip. On the other hand, if the cable has too much "slack," the clutch will not disengage sufficiently. While this may seem such an obvious problem, it is common. If the clutch is allowed to slip it will overheat and eventually destroy the discs. If the clutch does not completely disengage, the constant pressure of forcing a shift can damage the transmission shifting mechanism.

When you're convinced the problem is in the clutch, then start with the shop manual and a place to lay the pieces in correct order during disassembly. The spring pressure plate will probably be actuated by a pushrod that runs through the gearbox input shaft. If this rod is bent even slightly, it can bind and cause problems. Lay the pushrod on something perfectly flat and roll it back and forth. If it looks bent, it probably is. If the ends are mushroomed or worn excessively (check the length against that shown in the shop manual, or against a new one at the dealer), replace the rod. It is not expensive, so plan on a new one if there is any doubt whatsoever. Make sure the pushrod is adjusted exactly as the manual says.

The springs that operate clutch discs are very important. Because they are so inexpensive it is recommended they be replaced when a clutch is being repaired. But be sure and get a "matched" set. Measure the length of springs at the parts counter and use those that are nearly identical in length. Also, if your shop manual shows the clutch pressure being set by spring tension adjustment, have the partsman calibrate the tension of your new spring set, getting individual springs within a few ounces of each other in tension. Springs that are not matched can, and do, cause clutch action to be erratic. Once you have the clutch assembled you can check for this possible condition by disengaging the clutch and cranking the transmission through several turns (with the kickstarter or by rotating the rear wheel). If the discs seem to wobble, spring tension is incorrect.

There is usually not much that can go wrong with the clutch assembly hubs and housings. When you have the clutch apart, very carefully inspect these units. If there is a crack in any part, that part should be replaced. Where the clutch plate tab connects with the housing (sometimes called a chain-wheel) the housing can become slightly worn from the continual working of the tab. This must be smoothed off with a file, otherwise the tab can hang-up when the unit is reassembled. If the original clutch discs are being used again, also clean up the edges of all disc tabs. Make sure that any part of the hub/housing assembly held together by screws or nuts and bolts is really tight. This is particularly important on British clutches.

Clutch assemblies come in either a "wet" or "dry" configuration, depending on the type of motorcycle. It seems to be purely a matter of engineering preference. The wet clutch is designed to pass heat from the clutch pack as quickly as possible, but dry clutches work equally as well. If the clutch assembly is of the wet type, the housing will be well sealed, something you must pay particular attention to when putting things back together. The kind of clutch oil you use is a personal matter, but most modern clutches use automatic transmission fluid quite well. The majority of problems that come from sticking wet clutches are caused by an oil that is too heavy.

On the subject of oil, be aware that you might come up against some apparent discrepancy between what shop manuals and dealers advise. While one may say use 90 weight lubricant in the transmission, the dealer may say use a 30–50 weight oil. The petroleum industry uses different terminology when talking about oil and lubes for gears. The 90 weight lube and 30 weight oil might be about the same, but will vary in viscosity according to temperature. Use whatever the dealer recommends. ATF (automatic transmission fluid) is sometimes recommended for use in both clutch and transmission (and often even in the primary chain area). While there is controversy over the load-carrying capabilities of ATF, many riders use it in the transmission with no ill effects. It certainly works well enough with ball and roller bearings, but it is not so good with any kind of sleeve bearing.

Clutch plates should all be thoroughly cleaned and inspected. If the disc surface appears glazed or discolored, suspect a problem of slippage. If the disc smells scorched, it indicates too much heat in the clutch, again caused by slippage. Replace any disc that has been attacked by heat. Also replace any disc that is warped. If the tabs on outer or inner circumference (driving or driven disc) are distorted badly, the disc should also be replaced. There are different types of discs, and you can have some choice in how soft or hard you want the clutch to shift. Softer material on the composition-faced discs will give smoother operation, but are not recommended for tough competition. On the other hand, the severe shocks of off-road riding can be absorbed by soft discs (some bikes have a certain amount of clutch slippage "built in" to absorb these shocks between rear wheel and engine). Tell the dealer what kind of riding you do and he will have a good recommendation.

You can buy special accessory discs through most motorcycle shops, and some of these have metal discs made of aluminum rather than steel. The aluminum is heat-treated, is usually stronger than the steel disc (which means less chance of warping), and now costs about the same as the steel replacement. Whether or not you use such an accessory will depend largely upon your type of riding, but it is an item worth consideration.

There are two types of connection between engine crankshaft and clutch/transmission. The primary chain system is merely that, a chain between the engine and clutch. This might be the traditional roller-type chain (the kind of chain used for final drive, similar to bicycle chain), or a new gear-type chain (a chain like that used between crankshaft gear and camshaft gear in a car). The gear type is still too new in use to get a good reading from the manufacturers, but if it works it will save a lot of headaches caused by roller primaries (mainly heat distortion and stretching). The second kind of connection is by a gear or gear train. Here a small gear on the crankshaft meshes directly with a large gear on the circumference of the clutch hub. This type of construction is common when the engine/transmission design is of the unit type (all together in one housing). The primary chain is used when the transmission is separate from the engine.

There are two ways torque can enter and leave a transmission. In the most obvious, power comes through chain or gear to the clutch, goes through the transmission to a sprocket on the opposite side of the gearbox and then via chain or driveshaft to the rear wheel. There are some peculiar bearing-loading problems with this type of power transfer, so the most popular method is to have the clutch input shaft run inside the output shaft. In this way, the final drive sprocket is between transmission housing and clutch assembly. There is little the owner can, or will, do about this design characteristic of his bike.

Although the owner might not be able to modify the gearbox (due to the type of drive involved), he can be fully aware of the advantages of each when he first selects a bike. For the manufacturer who might want to make some significant changes in a particular line, the separate gearbox is preferable. That is, if a twin-cylinder engine is to be fitted to a frame originally using a single-cylinder engine, it is obviously less costly if a separate gearbox already in use can be retained. Such simplicity, and consequent reduction in owner cost, should not go overlooked. Further, if some form of competition is involved, the owner will find it much easier to remove the engine and leave the gearbox in place (that is, in the frame) for minor repairs.

Motorcycle gearboxes are amazingly strong and agile components, considering the very difficult design limitations of weight and size. The gears are made of either a direct-hardening steel, or a case-hardening steel, in both cases the result is a very tough gear at low cost. Because the gear shafts are subject to a requirement for bending resistance rather than steel hardness, they may not be the total quality the gears are. This is of little consequence to the owner, unless his bike consistently has shaft failure problems. If a problem occurs, it will probably be improper shaft alignment rather than poor shaft material or construction. Any recurring problem in the gearbox should be submitted to a good motorcycle repair service, where the gearbox housing can be checked thoroughly for shaft bore and bearing alignment.

The gearbox shifting mechanism will vary widely between different motorcycle makes, but the principle will always remain the same, that is, to move a sliding gear the minimum distance with the least resistance. To this end a considerable number of different designs have been utilized, but the English type with two separate shifter forks operated independently is a favorite. Of importance to the rider is the inherent strength of his particular shifting mechanism. Before engaging in any kind of competition or rough off-road riding, he should consult the bike shop and learn about any peculiarities of his gearbox, and how strong the shifting mechanism is. A little tip that might save a long walk out of the boondocks.

The transmission built integrally with the engine housing will be stronger, generally, than the separate gearbox, and is usually designed to reduce weight and production costs. Whichever type of transmission is employed, it is important to use the correct transmission fluid, and it is imperative that the fluid be kept clean. Should dirt get into the gearbox, it will soon ruin the gear-teeth clearances, which are critical to smooth box operation, and the bearings will fail in a short time.

A small oil spot caused by the transmission may or may not be a characteristic of a specific design. Some gearboxes will leak ever so slightly no matter how much assembly care is used; others will never leak no matter how badly the mechanic does the job. Again, it is wise to confer with the motorcycle shop as to what you can expect from a given make of bike. If there is a rather large pool of oil left wherever the bike is parked, something isn't right. Usually this will be nothing more than a seal, but it can be trouble with the housing mating surfaces, and it definitely should be cured. Haul the box to a mechanic if you can't find the problem; don't let it go unsolved.

Although there are a few shaft-drive motorcycles available, most notably the German BMW, the vast majority of bikes use chain final drive (and chain primaries), so we'll limit our final-drive discussion to chains and sprockets. Unfortunately, it is impossible to really consider either chain or sprocket individually, since each has a direct bearing on the condition and operation of the other. Let's look at the chain first.

Chain sizes are classified by pitch and width measurement, which means a ⅝ by ⅜ chain has a pitch of ⅝ inch and a width of ⅜ inch. Pitch is the distance between the link-pin centers, the most common being ⅜, ½, and ⅝ inch. Width is the roller width and distance between the links (approximate) and will be slightly more than the sprocket width for running clearance. Typical widths will vary from ⅛ to ⅜ inch. When you're talking about chain length, you're counting the number of pitches (total of inside and outside links).

Two kinds of links are in a motorcycle chain: pin and roller. The pin link is that part which has the two solid pins pressed into side links (the outside links). The roller links are pieces of tubular bushing material pressed into sideplates (the inside links) into which the pin link fits. The roller link fits the sprocket teeth, the pin link holds everything together (a master link is a pin link). The roller part fits over an inner bushing that presses into the sideplate and is free to revolve, the pin fits through this same bushing and allows the chain to bend. The rollerless chain obviously doesn't have the roller and is used in places where there is very low power transmittal. Be aware that there is a special link for varying chain length only one link (usually you must change two links at a time). This is called an "offset" link and is available at all bike shops.

Lubrication is where most chains die, especially those ridden exclusively on the street. The primary chain may not be a problem if it is enclosed with a wet clutch (oil should just cover the lower section of chain), but with a dry clutch the oil level must always be checked often. If the primary chain is not enclosed, there may be a "drip" tube that lets a bit of oil drip onto the chain during operation. It is essential that this system always be operative. If there is no method of oiling the primary chain, it should be generously lubricated with oil every 200 or 300 miles. Special chain lube is available at most bike shops for the purpose.

Lubrication requirements of the rear chain will depend entirely on how the motorcycle is used. Some road bikes have a chain oiler and this will be sufficient for the average street machine where only a light oiling is necessary (if no oiler is fitted, you'll have to do it with an oil can occasionally), If the bike is ridden off the highway even a slight amount, dirt will stick to the chain oil, so adding oil over this dirt mixture may only accelerate chain and sprocket wear. Most riders prefer to remove the rear chain and clean it thoroughly in solvent (do not use gasoline, for the sake of safety!), then soak the chain in heated oil for maximum lubricant penetration. If you do this on a bike which has a slightly enclosed rear-chain drive sprocket, you can save frustrating reassembly time by using a second piece of chain (used chain works fine). Split the chain in use and hook on the length of used chain, rotate until this second chain is on the enclosed sprocket, then remove the good chain and clean. To reassemble, hook to the used chain and pull through the sprocket and remove the used chain. Works neat.

If you don't want to remove the chain for this kind of maximum lubrication (which should be done every 1,000 dirt miles, or more often in extreme conditions), raise the rear wheel and rotate the chain while cleaning with solvent and a brush, then squirt on oil or special chain lube.

A chain will wear 200 or 300 percent faster when it is dry, so always keep it lubed. When it does get dry, the metal pieces can actually weld themselves together, and then tear apart, a condition known as "galling," and a situation that should be avoided. Galling can result from no lubricant, too thin an oil so that it breaks down in use, and too thick an oil that won't penetrate all portions of the roller and pin bushing. It is also possible for the chain loads to be so high the lube is actually squeezed out of the contact point.

The most ordinary chain oil is SAE 20, 30, and 40 motor oil; thin for cold weather, thicker for hot weather. More recently special chain lubricants have been marketed that are better than oil (which resists rust rather poorly) and better than boiling the chain in oil. They come in spray cans. Typical of this type is Ashland Chain Lube, which foams out white and seems to flow into every possible nook and cranny. LPS 3 is especially good, also, as it can be applied when the chain is wet (as after a good spray cleaning with water and detergent) and will adhere to the metal before the metal has a chance to rust.

When applying this type of lube, or plain oil, jack up the rear wheel and put the lube on the sprocket. This allows it to get down into the bushings without flying all over everything, but remember to do both sides of the sprocket to be sure you get lube throughout the bushing.

Chains will fail from a number of reasons, but normal wear from use will cause replacement that must be anticipated. While a primary chain may get between 20,000 and 30,000 miles' use if it is lubricated and adjusted properly, the rear chain will usually get no more than 15,000 miles under normal conditions. An off-road bike will almost never get chain life anywhere near this good.

Every chain will be designed for an ultimate tensile strength, or its ability to take a steady pull, but this kind of failure is not common during use. Fatigue failure is not uncommon, however, and is caused by the loads applied to the various chain pieces. These loads can be really severe, as when the rear wheel touches the ground after a jump. A fatigue crack in the sideplate usually shows as a hairline crack that starts at the bushing or pinhole and works outward. The bushings can have fatigue cracks, too, but in all cases it is best to replace the chain. If there are visible cracks in a few links, chances are they are elsewhere, but unseen. A tight joint is a form of fatigue problem (two link sideplates rub against one another), and must be cured. Look for high loads, something rubbing

**103**

against the chain, poor lubrication, or misaligned sprockets with this kind of fatigue. Sprocket misalignment shows as wear on one side of the sprocket. Eyeball the chain from the rear and you'll usually spot this misalignment (improper rear-wheel adjustment, swing-arm bent, drive sprocket installed backward, wrong shims on the sprockets, etc.).

The only way you can really tell how much a chain is worn is to measure the length and compare this to original length. Since this original measurement may not be available, relative length can be checked. Lay the chain on the floor and stretch it out completely. Mark both ends on the floor. Now hold one end and push the chain together, making another mark to show compressed length. If the difference is less than 3 percent of the total chain length, with normal sprockets, the chain is ok. If you are running an unusually large rear sprocket, the percentage will be closer to 2.5, so in this case better check with the bike shop to make sure. All this works out to ⅛ to 3/16 inch per foot maximum.

Another quick way to check chain wear, assuming the sprocket is not worn excessively, is to grasp the chain at the rearmost portion as it wraps around the sprocket and lift it off the sprocket. If it can be lifted more than one-half the height of the sprocket teeth (or more), it is worn out. Although the worn chain can be used, it will accelerate sprocket wear, so you lose more money in the long run by trying to get extra mileage from a bad chain.

A chain-breaker is a simple, inexpensive little tool that every bike rider should keep in his emergency kit. It makes repairs far easier than pliers and vise-grips and files. Master links may be the press-fit or spring-clip type; the former are better if you're going to be in competition. If a press-fit master link is used, you'll definitely want the chain-breaker along.

Chain adjustment has a direct bearing on loads imposed on the chain, so it is vital to check this adjustment often and modify it as the chain stretches. For a bike with a plunger-type rear end, slack should be ⅜ to ½ inch with the rear wheel jacked up, or ¾ to 1 inch with the rider seated. This is an up-and-down slack. A swinging arm frame would call for an unloaded slack of 1¼ to 1½ inches, while loaded the slack would be about ¾ inch minimum. A rigid frame would have a ¾-inch slack minimum. Primary chain slack would be ⅜ to ½ inch.

You can get special chains, but these are primarily for special applications, such as serious racing, and they are not inexpensive. Anytime you buy a used bike, bet on the chain being poor and the sprockets being wasted. Plan on buying both sprockets and chain before you're happy on the road.

Sprockets are a thing unto themselves, and the amateur mechanic usually gets into trouble in only two ways: he tries to use worn sprockets with new chain (which accelerates new chain wear), or he mismatches sprockets (size, chain type, or manufacture). When replacing sprockets, always buy matched sets and never use a used and a new sprocket together.

The kind of mileage you can expect from a sprocket will depend on the use of your motorcycle, and on the kind of bike you have. Lightweight bikes with the small sprocket on the gearbox drive may not get even 10,000 miles, while the steel sprocket is always better than the cast-iron type (which may get only 5,000 miles). Primary sprockets usually get much better mileage, usually in the neighborhood of 30,000 to 40,000 miles, so they can be changed with primary chains.

The main point to remember about replacing sprockets is not to bend the unit when removing it, especially if a puller is used with a tapered-shaft design. If the sprocket is riveted to the base, use replacement rivets of the correct diameter and length (about $\frac{3}{32}$ inch should extend for riveting). Bolt-on sprockets are no problem, but splined sprockets may tend to loosen the bolt if the splines are not a tight fit. Some Loc-tite will work to keep both the nut and the splined area secure.

You can get into all kinds of trouble by messing with the gearing ratio, a ratio that is changed by altering the number of teeth on a sprocket. Some trail bikes have an auxiliary large sprocket bolted to the standard road sprocket. This gives the very low gearing desirable for mountain climbing. Generally speaking, however, the average rider will want to stick with the same gearing the bike was originally produced with. In the event a change in ratio is desired for competition, it is advisable to confer with someone who already races. There is much to be considered when changing the gear ratio, such as the type of racing, tire sizes and style, rider handling technique, engine power band, and so on.

Most bikes have four sprockets in the drive train, plus the gears in the transmission; thus the final ratio will depend on the number of teeth on all four sprockets and the number of teeth in the transmission. To get the final gear ratio in high gear, first divide the primary sprockets, next divide the final drive sprockets, and multiply the two answers. For example, a Harley XLCH has 34 teeth at the engine, 59 teeth at the clutch, 20 teeth at the transmission, and 51 teeth at the rear wheel. 59 divided by 34 is 1.735. 51 divided by 20 is 2.550. Multiply the answers and you get a final ratio of 4.424:1. A similar close estimate will come by jacking up the rear wheel and counting the number of crankshaft revolutions to one rear-wheel revolution. To get transmission ratios, multiply final ratio times transmission gear ratio.

It is essential to follow the instructions in the specific motorcycle repair manual when working on clutches and transmissions, otherwise it is possible to get pieces together incorrectly. Follow all torque specifications, and always use new parts if there is any doubt as to drivetrain condition.

# Motorcycle Brakes

When the first motorcycles were being built before the turn of the century, brakes were the stirrup type already in use. These early brakes pressed two pads against the sides of the wheel rim, exerting little braking force on machines twice the weight of ordinary bicycles. To put it mildly, they were terrible!

As early as 1897, efforts were being made to find suitable materials for brake linings and surfaces. By 1910 brake surfacings had been improved to the point that the first practical braking systems were being built for motorcycles. Like most of the other motorcycle parts of those days, the brakes were still too light for the horsepower that was being developed, but the basic designs that would be used for half a century (until the advent of the disc brake on production motorcycles) were at last being used.

Let's define exactly what we mean by a motorcycle

brake. It is a device that reverses the process performed by the engine. The internal-combustion engine takes a mixture of air and fuel, compresses it, then burns it to create a powerful expanding gas which pushes on the pistons to provide a driving force to propel the motorcycle. The brake in turn removes this driving force from the motorcycle, dissipating it in the form of heat. More simply stated, the friction between a brake shoes or pad and the moving surface of a drum or disc interferes with the free movement of the rotating part, causing it to slow down. The energy that is removed from the rotating mass is given off in the form of heat, and as this chapter will show, heat is the problem in designing or using any braking system effectively on a motorcycle.

In addition to better materials and design of the brakes themselves, recent advances in tire construction and rubber compounds have had an effect on the ability of motorcycle braking systems. It is now possible to buy a motorcycle that is capable of stopping at rates that would have been considered impossible only ten years ago. This is of interest to the beginning rider because these high-performance bikes with their powerful acceleration and quick stopping can be a dangerous handful for the inexperienced.

The technique of using motorcycle brakes effectively is different from that of an automobile. The average car has many times the tire contact area on the ground, and only a single control to provide braking force. The motorcycle has only a very small amount of rubber on the ground to maintain stability, and two separate controls which act to give precise control in the hands of an expert rider.

The front brake of a motorcycle provides the most braking action due to the transfer of weight forward under braking. It is controlled by a hand lever mounted on the right handlebar and is used by the same hand that controls the throttle. On paved surfaces and traveling in a straight line, the front brake should provide the most effective stopping power, but because it acts quicker and stronger than the rear brake, some finesse is needed. The front brake should never be jerked hard in a panic stop unless the rider is willing to take the chance of finding himself sliding down the highway on his side.

Balanced braking is the key to riding a motorcycle well. The rear brake does not provide as much stopping force, but is necessary to retain control during stopping. Under normal circumstances the best technique is to apply the rear brake a split second before the front. This stabilizes the bike in the direction of travel and makes it much less apt to want to swap ends. Smooth and steady use of the brakes comes naturally after a few weeks of riding, and only the rawest beginner will find himself mentally hesitating before using the brakes with the same sureness that he does in his car. One thing that would make the whole process a lot easier and something that this writer has advocated for years is standardization of brake-lever placement on all motorcycles. The rear brake is actuated by a foot lever, and while most Japanese bikes use a pattern of brake lever on the right and shifter on the left, English machines and one major American bike have the opposite setup with the brake lever underneath the left foot. Since braking, like most other actions, is not carried out by conscious thought in an emergency, riding a bike with a brake-lever position that is unfamiliar can cause serious problems. The whole thing might be quite safe until some problem causes the rider to act quickly. Then established reactions take over, and instead of braking safely to a stop, the rider winds up in trouble. Hopefully some form of private agreement or government regulation will get the manufacturers to standardize this in the near future.

Riding on paved surfaces usually means that braking will be precise and without variation, unlike off-road riding where the surface changes from place to place, and with it braking conditions. But there are a couple of things the street rider should be aware of. One is the presence of gravel or sand on the road surface. This presents a dangerous problem to the rider who may suddenly round a corner to find that a layer of gravel from a dirt side road extends into the lane in which he is traveling. If the rider is moving fast and leaning over quite a bit in cornering, he may find himself going down without ever touching the brakes. But braking when leaning the bike or on uncertain surfaces is a sure bet for an accident.

The brakes can be used when you are leaned over in a turn, but caution is the word. The good rider will try if possible to select a line through a turn that will allow him to complete his braking before actually entering the turn, so he can exit the turn under power. If he finds that he must use the brakes in the turn, he will either use them lightly when leaned over or widen the radius of the turn and bring the bike to a more upright stance before getting on the brakes hard.

There is no more beautiful sight in the world than a fine rider taking a well-built motorcycle swiftly through a series of turns along a mountain road. Man and motorcycle are as one, dipping and rising on each corner. If you watch the rider carefully, you will notice that he covers ground rapidly without obvious effort. Smoothness is the key. By following him you can watch how he lines the bike up for each corner, downshifting and braking on the way into the corner, holding a steady speed through the central part, then accelerating quickly out of the last portion of the curve. At no time will he use the brakes after he is leaned over in the curve unless something such as oncoming traffic forces him to deviate from the line he has selected.

For the beginner it is this smoothness in braking and accelerating that is so hard to master. You must learn to ride mentally ahead of the bike, anticipating the conditions that lie ahead. Learn to read the surface of the road. Shiny spots or stains indicate the presence of oil or water that could turn braking into a skid. Never ride in the exact center of a travel lane when stopping at an intersection. Drippings from automobile engines destroy the asphalt and create a potential hazard area just before the white line of the crosswalk. The painted lines themselves are an area to be avoided, they are slippery, especially when wet, and can cause a slide or skid if you put the brakes on while the tires are on the paint. Your surroundings can tell you a lot about the conditions you can expect to find around the next curve. In places where construction is going on there is every possibility of loose materials on the road. If you are riding in the early morning or evening, beware of land-scaped center dividers and road edges. Automatic sprinkler systems can often cause wet pavement areas and riders have been injured by just such things. Braking a motorcycle on wet pavement is not as hard as it looks provided the rider is careful not to overuse the brakes. It is, however, much easier to get a skid started on wet ground, and again smoothness is the word. Wet highways, even in heavy rain, are fairly safe for motorcycle use if approached with understanding and experience. Many riders who specialize in cross-country touring by bike come prepared for bad weather and think nothing of riding for hundreds of miles in rain. It's mostly a matter of knowing what to expect.

Off-road riding requires a completely different approach to motorcycle braking. When riding in the dirt, the rider must expect that any hard braking will be accompanied by sliding of the tire. A good dirt rider will anticipate the point at which he wants to stop and begin braking earlier than he would on pavement. The front brake is not used as much when riding in the dirt, as in pavement riding. The reason is simple, a sliding front wheel does not provide any directional control, and the front brake will lock up the front wheel much easier in dirt. Many riders adjust the front brake control so they only get a fraction of normal braking from a strong pull on the lever. This keeps them from having to stop and think about how much pressure should be applied to the lever while bouncing along over rough terrain.

The rear brake is the most effective in dirt, although there is a limit to how much braking force can be applied with either brake in loose earth. When negotiating a steep hill, use engine compression and gearing to provide most of the braking action. Use the rear brake only as much as necessary and be careful not to get it locked up. Moving your body weight aft over the rear tire is helpful when going down a steep grade such as an embankment or hill. The increased weight over the rear tire will let you use more braking action. Two-stroke bikes which do not provide much in the way of compression braking can be equipped with a hand-controlled device called a compression release. This little gadget vents the cylinder to outside air when the lever is pulled, increasing the braking ability of the engine.

The brakes on all dirt bikes are good enough for off-road use, but many of the smaller dual-purpose machines have such tiny brakes that riding them on pavement to and from the dirt can be hazardous unless the rider is aware that they don't stop very well and acts accordingly. Together with the compression release on the two-stroke bike, and careful selection of gears for off-road use, the braking of most dirt bikes is easy to learn in just a few trips to the dirt. Unlike pavement riding where the idea is to avoid skidding the tire, there are instances where the dirt rider will deliberately lock up one or both tires to start a slide. By knowing just how and where to slide the bike under both power and brake, the good off-road rider can cover ground much quicker, seeming to be almost constantly sliding sideways from one turn to another. A well set-up broadslide is an effective way to stop in a hurry, but it is a maneuver that is best let alone until you have learned some of the basics of off-road riding.

One of the hardest things for the fledgling off-road rider to learn when trying to ride a bike down a steep hill is that it's safer to be going a little too fast than it is to try and go too slow. Once the bike starts down the hill, gravity will keep it going even with both brakes locked up solid. Once the front brake is locked, you have lost all directional control and will probably arrive at the bottom with the bike on top of you. It's much better to move a bit faster, letting the suspension take up the shocks and using the brakes only lightly to maintain control and position. When you reach the bottom and run out on level ground, then brake down to the speed you wish to travel.

Beginning riders have a tendency to ride beyond the limit of their ability to stop. When you first venture off paved roads into soft ground remember that conditions have changed and forceful braking is as bad as hitting the thing you were trying to avoid. When applying the brakes while traveling in a straight line on gravel or dirt, move your weight aft over the rear tire to offiset weight transfer somewhat and be alert for the start of sideways motion that signals the beginning of an out-of-control situation. The brakes can be used with somewhat more authority when leaned over on a bike being ridden in dirt than on hard surfaces. Most knobby tires have a considerable tread surface high on the side of the tire and will give excellent traction even when the bike is pitched over at a sharp angle.

Most dirt bikes have brakes that are well sealed against dirt and water, but if you are out trail riding with friends and have to ford a stream that is deep enough to cover the brake drums, ride carefully for the next few minutes until the brakes have had a chance to dry out. This writer once wound up at the bottom of a wash because he neglected to check for brakes that had just been thoroughly wetted in a stream crossing. The same thing can happen on a street bike that his just been washed.

Until recently all but one of the motorcycle manufacturers equipped their bikes with mechanical brakes operated by cables. Only Harley-Davidson's huge touring bike had a hydraulic brake, and that was only on the rear wheel. Things have changed. With the explosion of the superbikes into the touring market with their fantastic acceleration potential, more and more bikes are being equipped with hydraulic disc brakes that are capable of stopping these fast machines quickly from speeds of well over 120 mph. Does that mean that the old-fashioned drum brake is out of the picture? Not at all. Some of the finest brakes used on racing bikes today are the Fontana drum assemblies with four shoes inside a single drum. Many other good drum brakes are available, and it will be a long time before any but the biggest and fastest bikes come equipped with disc brakes.

Modern drum brakes are of the internal expanding type. Years ago many motorcycles were equipped with external brakes that contracted to apply pressure, but these had the serious disadvantage of exposed workings that were susceptible to water and rust. And they were ugly to boot!

Two types of braking action comprise the majority of brakes: self-energizing, which means the brakes are designed so that once the brake shoe comes in contact with the surface of the drum, the rotation forces the shoe in against the drum and enhances the braking effect; and nonenergizing, which produces no addtional braking force. (Disc brakes are nonenergizing, which is the reason so many of them are power-assisted on cars.)

A brake shoe that produces this additional braking force is called a leading shoe, one that does not is a trailing shoe. Normally the front brake on a motorcycle will contain a pair of leading shoes, and the rear brake will have a single leading shoe or one leading and one trailing. This is because the rear brake cannot use effectively as much force as the front and reduction of its braking power prevents locking up the rear wheel as easily. A number of specialized racing drum brakes have been developed for motorcycle racing, and some contain as many as four leading shoes, giving unbelievable stopping power.

You'll recall that we pointed out at the beginning of this chapter that the brake transformed the energy of the bike's forward motion into heat. A great amount of research has gone into brake compounds and linings, all aimed at two specific tasks. One is coming up with a compound that gives good stopping power, the other to combine that stopping power with reliability and long wear. Reliability is a matter of brake fade, which means that as the brakes are used several times in rapid succession, they heat up until the material no longer functions as a friction device. This causes the brake to lose effectiveness and "fade." If the rider slows his pace and allows the brakes to cool for a few minutes they will return to their original effectivness. Brake linings that have high resistance to fading are often made of such a hard material that until the brakes have been used a few times, stopping is not as good as it should be. Racing brakes are normally like this. Designed to stop a speeding motorcycle from speeds of 150 mph or more, they do not work well on the street. There are brake linings that offer exceptional stopping ability plus the ability to stop well when cold, but again a compromise is made. In order to get a lining that stops quickly even when cold, the material is usually soft and wears quickly. You can see that brakes are a lot of different things depending on the use to which a bike will be put.

Several things are done to improve the fade resistance of drum brakes. Air scoops are used in the sides of the brake backing plate to bring in outside air for cooling. Some even have extra surface area in the form of cast fins to radiate heat away from the brake. In a couple of racing brakes, angled fins are cast into the drum to act as a fan to pull air through the brake drum so that more cooling can be obtained.

The disc brake is coming into more use in production motorcycles these days, with almost every top-of-the-line road machine sporting the disc and caliper on the front end. Because the disc brake does not have the self-energizing effect of a leading-shoe unit, most of the disc assemblies offered for sale are hydraulic. This provides the necessary force multiplication to make the brake work. The disc brake has several advantages over the drum brake. One is that because the disc is nonenergizing it will allow more sensitive control of braking. It's almost impossible to lock up a disc brake under normal conditions. Another factor in favor of the disc is that more cooling air can reach the brake lining material.

Honda was the first to introduce the disc to the United States on a production motorcycle, with their fabulous 750 Four. The brake consists of a single steel disc mounted on the left side of the front wheel, and a caliper containing two pads of brake material on the left front fork leg. A hydraulic line runs from the caliper to the master cylinder/lever on the right handlebar. When the lever is pulled, the hydraulic action forces the two pads of brake material against the spinning steel disc, slowing the bike rapidly.

Many of the new breed of superbikes have disc brakes, and their use on racing bikes of all kinds and sizes is growing. Recently the king heavyweight of motorcycles, the Harley-Davidson 74 which had been equipped with the only hydraulic rear brake on a motorcycle, became the first bike to use hydraulic brakes on both wheels. The front brake is a huge disc that increases the stopping power of this heavy machine by a tremendous amount. Others using the disc are the Suzuki 750, the Yamaha 650 Twin, the new Honda 500-cc Four, and many other smaller bikes. It's clear that the disc is here to stay in motorcycling.

## Maintenance

Repair and servicing of the brakes on your bike is a task that is easy for most riders, even those who normally don't think of themselves as mechanics. With the exception of the Harley 74, none of the motorcycles has a rear brake with a hydraulic cylinder that must be rebuilt like those on a car. On bikes that have a control rod running from the brake pedal to the lever on the backing plate, adjustment for pedal travel is necessary whenever the rear wheel is moved to adjust drive-chain tension. Adjustment is easy; just screw in or out the spring-loaded nut that holds the rod to the lever. One point here: many wise dirt riders will move the brake pedal upward as much as possible to lessen the chance of the pedal or their foot catching on brush or rocks. It's no fun having a rock or twig put the brake on for you when you're traveling at high speed over rough terrain.

The front brake on most bikes is adjustable by a pair of jam nut adjusters on either end of the brake cable. A tip here again for you prospective dirt riders: adjust the front brake until it just starts to work at the very end of the lever pull. This works better for two reasons. First, the brake is harder to lock up, preventing loss of control; second, you can hold the lever partly depressed under a couple of fingers, allowing you to use the brake a bit without having to release your grip on the handlebars. This can be a blessing when you're riding hard over bumpy ground.

Unless you own the same bike for several years or have a big road bike that gets thousands of miles put on it every year, chances are you'll never have any reason to do anything to the brakes except adjust them from time to time. They wear surprisingly well on most bikes. If you do get the urge to work on them, get the service manual for the particular bike. On most drum-brake bikes, rebuilding is simply a matter of taking the brakes apart, checking the drums to see if there is any scoring or pitting in the drum surface, installing new linings and putting the whole thing back together. If the drum surface is scored or out of round, the shop will turn the drum in a lathe to true it, and sell you a set of oversize linings to fit. Then just put them together. On drum-brake Harleys the linings are not just exchanged. The old lining is taken off the shoe and new ones are riveted in place, a job best left to the shop mechanic who has the proper tools.

The most frequent job on brakes will be checking and replacing worn or broken brake cables. These have a way of breaking way out in the middle of nowhere just as the sun goes down. Most factory brake cables have a soldered-on end that fits into the lever housing or arm on the backing plate. Take my advice and always carry a couple of the screw-on ends and a small wrench to repair such problems. A short length of strong wire will also make a good traveling companion. I've used wire several times on everything from broken brake and clutch cables to strengthening a badly cracked frame until I could slowly and carefully ride out of the desert.

On disc brakes, unless you have some experience with automotive hydraulic brakes or are willing to get your hands dirty learning, I advise you to take them to a qualified service man for repair. One of the things that make discs slightly more complicated to work on is that they require very clean disassembly and working areas to avoid getting dirt inside the moving parts of the calipers. The sides of the disc should be checked for warpage and scoring, just like the inside surface of a drum brake. The pads of brake material are changed when worn out just as are the brake shoes. One thing is easier on disc brakes. It's often possible to measure the pad thickness without removing any parts, and because the sides of the disc are in plain view, it's easier to keep track of the condition of the metal portion of the brake. Servicing a hydraulic disc is mostly confined to making sure the fluid reservoir is full of the correct type of hydraulic brake fluid, and checking once in a while for leaks in the hoses and fittings.

For the most part, motorcycle brakes are trouble-free. Once a rider learns how to use them correctly in all situations, they will give him fresh confidence in his ability to ride his way out of dangerous situations and will increase his enjoyment in motorcycling as both a sport and practical transportation.

# Tires and Wheels

The selection of the correct tire-wheel combination for the type of riding you intend to do with your motorcycle can be more important to your enjoyment and riding safety than any other item. Therein lies a problem for the beginning rider. There are so many types of tires and rims, each with a specific function, that unless careful consideration is made when buying, you may find yourself spending additional cash for a different set of tires before the ones that came on the bike are showing signs of wear.

Although each phase of the motorcycle sport has a group of tires intended just for that type of activity, all motorcycle tires are manufactured in the same way. The tire starts life as a pattern of cords placed in a mold into which rubber is poured in a hot molding process. The mold forms the tread pattern on the outside of the tire while the molten rubber is bonding itself to the cord to form the fin-

ished tire. The cords are strings of various materials, sometimes nylon or rayon, or in some new tires fiberglass. Each
layer of cord is called a ply (tires are rated by plies, 2 ply,
4 ply, etc.) and the number of plies in the tire indicates its
strength. The angle at which the cords lay across the tire
determines the use of the tire. A tire for street use may
have two plies, and the angle of the plies will normally be
between 38 and 40 degrees. Decreasing the cord angle, as
in road-racing tires, to around 28 to 30 degrees will give a
better cornering tire for competition use, but this tire demands a little extra skill on the part of the rider. That
brings up an important point: don't use pure racing tires
on the street. They have been designed for racing purposes
only, and while they may give better handling, they are
not suited for long wear and can be dangerous in street
use.

The edge of the tire that fits inside the rim is called the
bead. The plies of cord that form the curved section of the
tire are tied together at this point and the bead has a series
of steel wires running around the tire's edge to help hold
the cords, and to keep the tire in contact with the rim at
all times. The area of the bead is the stiffest and strongest
part of the tire because of these steel wires, which is one
of the reasons the tire is so hard to get on and off the wheel.

The rubber compound that is molded to the cords in
each tire is another area where tires designed for specific
purposes differ. Racing tires will normally have a compound that lasts for only a short time, often wearing away

completely during the course of a single race, but giving much more traction than is found in a street tire whose harder rubber lasts much longer. Tires designed for off-road use will have very hard compounds because the tire must take such hard abuse. The best tire for the average motorcycle use is one that gives good mileage to keep the cost of motorcycling down, yet still has enough flex and traction to provide a comfortable and safe ride.

Unless you are a serious racer or something of an engineer, cord angle or tire compound won't mean much to you when buying a tire. The two things that will be important are tire size and tread design. Tire-size requirements can differ widely depending on the use being made of the motorcycle. If the bike is to be used strictly for street and highway use, often the manufacturers' recommendations are the best bet. They spend a lot of time trying to come up with tires that are compatible with the suspension on their road bikes, and unless you're sure that a change is in order or have some specific reason for changing tire sizes, leave them alone.

There is a general rule that can be followed for off-road bikes and tire sizes. Use as large a tire (width or cross section) as will fit the rear swingarm and clear the chain. A bike of 175 cc's or less will normally wind up with a tire of 3.00 to 3.50 cross-section, and the bigger bikes, which also develop much more power to handle a larger-width tire, will use a 4.00 to 4.50 size. On the front, a change in both tire width and diameter is often helpful in off-road use. A great many experienced riders will remove the 18- or 19-inch front tire and wheel, replacing them with a 21-inch unit. The larger diameter of the front wheel allows it to roll over rocks and holes that would trap a smaller tire and wheel, sometimes causing a spill. This 21-inch tire/ wheel setup works best on true off-road bikes. If you do most of your riding off-pavement, but usually on graded fire roads or gravel forest-service paths, stick to the 19-inch tire diameter with a fatter cross-section. The ground is much harder and the loose top cover will sometimes cause the narrow, tall, 21-incher to wash out or slide easily.

Tread design is just as important as size. There are three basic types of tread designs for motorcycle tires: road or touring tires which have a smooth tread much like that on an automobile tire; off-road tires, called "knobbies" because they have a raised block-pattern tread that gives good traction in soft dirt or sand; and the in-between or universal tire with elements of both treads in the design. The road tire is just that, a road tire. It is not intended to be used in the dirt, and side excursions down unpaved roads can be dangerous and costly if the rider is not careful. Tread patterns in road tires vary from a simple ribbed design to complex block types and in some cases rain tires for bad-weather operation. One interesting point about some of the block-pattern road tires with a soft compound is that they make pretty good fire-road tires for the guy who likes to play-race and broadslide the bike through the turns. They will give good traction and are predictable at the point of breakaway, but that's about the only use of a road tire I would recommend in dirt riding. Stay out of the soft stuff with street tires!

The pure off-road tire has a hard compound and a heavy knobbed surface to get maximum bite in sand and soft dirt. If road tires have their limits, the same is even more true of knobbies. Don't ride on pavement with knobby tires unless you have to. The knobby tire does not offer much in the way of traction on hard paved surfaces and any mistake usually results in a crash. If you must use a section of highway while going from one dirt riding area to another, ride carefully.

Out in the rough stuff the knobby tire shines. The protruding hunks of rubber bite deeply into the loose surface and very little wheelspin results from all but the most violent throttle action. Tread design of knobby tires differs somewhat, with a few types being manufactured for hard clay surfaces such as speedway tracks, but in general they are all the same except for the size of the knobs on the tire. Some well-known racers alter the tread by cutting different patterns on the knobs with a razor blade, but for the average rider the knobby is good just the way it comes from the factory. One point should be made: knobby tires are usually run at extremely low pressures to get even better traction, and some means of fastening the tire firmly to the rim should be used. Some riders prefer drilling the edge of the rim and using small sheet-metal screws to keep the tire from rotating on the rim, but most use a device called a rim lock. The rim on an off-road bike will have a couple of extra holes in it in addition to the valve stem hole. This is where the rim lock bolt comes out of the tire. The lock is a curved metal clamp that fits inside the tire and when tightened pinches the bad of the tire between the lock and the rim. A couple of these mounted on the rear tire and tightened pinches the bead of the tire between the lock and the and tearing off the valve stem. A good suggestion for those of you who ride hard in the dirt is an alignment mark of paint or ink on both tire and rim so that slippage can be detected at a glance and fixed before you find yourself stranded in the middle of nowhere with a flat.

The universal is a compromise tire, designed to be used for limited off-road riding and street use. To be frank, it doesn't do either as well as the correct tire for the job, but unless you are after total performance in the dirt, the universal will work all right. Most dual-purpose bikes come equipped with these universal tires, and if you know that you will not be using the bike on pavement, tell the salesman you want something different put on the bike before you take it. It will cost less that way than trying to find a pair of slightly used tires. In the universal category there are several different tread designs. Some are almost full knobbies, and others resemble a street tire closely, but are usually of a softer compound.

Installing and repairing motorcycle tires is different from automobile tire repair. Outside the motorcycle shop, chances are you won't find anybody who will fix or install the tire for you. Gas stations just don't have the tools for the job. Get used to carrying the tools on your bike and fix anything that goes wrong yourself. Most motorcycles come with a small tool kit that is supposed to allow the rider to fix small troubles alongside the highway. The painful truth is that most of the supplied kits are worthless. Make up a kit of your own or buy one made for enduro competition. There are several really good kits on the market and your dealership or off-road-bike specialty shop should be able to sell you one. They have been developing these kits for quite a while and some of them are so complete you could almost overhaul the bike under a tree. The riders who compete in enduro events and European trials can change a tire completely and repair it in less than five minutes with one of these tool kits.

If you should damage a tire so badly that it cannot be repaired on the spot and you're way out in the middle of nowhere, remove the tube and try stuffing the inside of the tire with grass or brush. I've seen a number of guys come all the way back to the pits in desert races with a tire full of brush. It's a lot better than sitting for hours waiting for somebody to find you. One other thing, don't ride off-road alone. Another pair of hands can be very helpful if something breaks, and should you crash and be hurt, having help close at hand could be the the difference between missing a few days' work and being laid up for a long time, or worse.

Normal tire servicing or repair is simple once you know

the techniques. Unless you're putting on a very heavy knobby tire, a pair of screwdrivers or the tire tools from the kit will be all that's required. Where the tire is large and has stiff sidewalls, a rubber hammer can be a big help. Be careful not to pinch the tube inside the tire when installing it. Put the tire on over one side of the rim, then carefully insert the tube with your fingers, smoothing it into place. Don't poke at it with a screwdriver or other sharp object, you'll just ruin the tube and have to start over. Make sure that the tube is not twisted inside the tire. Pull the valve stem through the hole in the rim and put the cap on; it will hold the stem in place. After the tube is in place the rim locks (if used) can be installed, but leave them loose so that both sides of the bead can be slid into position between the rim and lock. When the tire is completely on the rim, inflate it until hard, then let the air out and tighten the rim locks. The tire can then be inflated to the correct pressure and the wheel installed on the bike.

Before installing the tire and tube, check the rim for burrs on the inside of the lip, and the rubber liner that covers the spoke heads. If the liner is bad, a few turns of black electrical tape will do the same job. If any of the spokes protrude too much into the rim, they should be filed or ground off so there is less chance of puncturing the tube.

A lot of riders are unwilling to work on the wheels of their bike because the wire wheel with its spokes seems to be difficult to understand compared with the steel disc wheels on automobiles. Nothing could be further from the truth. The motorcycle wire wheel is a fairly simple device that almost anyone can take apart and put back together in his own garage, provided he uses a little common sense. The major problem with the wire wheel is that the spokes do loosen up after use and should be checked at frequent intervals. The harder the bike is ridden, the more often you should check for loose or broken spokes or damaged rims. For street bikes, a monthly half hour should be enough; dirt bikes should be checked at weekly intervals if ridden hard.

Motorcycle wheels are made of two materials, steel and an aluminum alloy. Both have their strong points, both have weaknesses. The steel rim is cheaper to buy, and has the advantage of holding chrome much better than the alloy rim. The disadvantages of steel rims are that mass-production methods frequently result in rims that are not quite round. Production tolerances of alloy rims are much closer and it's unusual to find one out of round from the factory. The steel rim is more likely to bend if subjected to a hard blow, as the alloy rim is stiffer. But the steel rim can be repaired if the damage is not too bad, whereas an alloy rim is ruined once it is badly bent (usually it breaks rather than bends). One other advantage of the alloy rim over steel is light weight. This is only important to the serious rider and off-road racer, but should be taken into consideration when planning a competition bike.

Rim widths are given by a series of WM numbers, a

WM-0 rim having an actual rim width of 2 inches, allowing installation of a tire from 2.25 to 2.50 inches in cross-section. On the other end of the scale is the WM-4 which, with an actual rim width of 4 inches, will take a 5- or 6-inch tire. There are larger rims in the works, some being entirely cast out of alloys, including the spokes (somewhat like the wheels used on racing cars). But for the average rider, most requirements will fall in the WM-0 to WM-4 range.

The spokes also have a size series expressed by comparing the spoke diameter with a steel-wire gauge. Most wheels will be laced at the factory with spokes of 8- to 12-gauge wire. Off-road wheels that are going to see a lot of punishing terrain will require heavier spokes in the 6-, 8-, or 10-gauge range. Road racers, striving to remove as much weight as possible from their bikes, will use very light 12-gauge spokes, actually figuring the spoke flex into the total suspension package for the bike!

The thin nuts that hold the spoke to the rim are called nipples and can be had in several metals. Most import bikes are equipped with brass nipples, but for heavy use nickle-plated steel nipples are advisable. If you're a weight-conscious racer, aluminum nipples will remove a couple of ounces from a wheel, but it's not worth it for the average rider.

The way the spokes are laced to the hub and rim determines how strong the finished wheel will be. Wheel lacers refer to the patterns as "cross one" or "cross three," etc., indicating how many spokes an individual spoke crosses between the rim and hub. The strongest pattern is a matter of debate even among experienced lacers, but generally the more spokes crossed by each spoke on its way from rim to hub, the stronger the wheel will be. In changing from one lacing pattern to another, you must remember that as the angle of the spoke increases, its length must also increase. This means that any pattern change will require a complete new set of spokes. I won't try to list all the combinations available; your parts man at the local cycle shop will be able to fix you up with the correct items if you should decide to lace a set of wheels yourself.

Before lacing a wheel, check the hub and rim to make sure that there are no worn spoke holes or dents and cracks in the rim. A steel rim that is not too badly bent can be straightened with a soft-faced hammer and a suitable backstop. Don't try to use an anvil, you'll just destroy the rim; instead try a piece of wood or some other softer material under the rim while you're pounding on it. Unless you can get the rim perfectly round again, it's generally not worth the trouble to straighten with a hammer. But if you are in a fix for cash or are a long way from home with a bent wheel, it's nice to know that it can be done.

To lace a wheel properly, certain tools are a must. A stand that will allow the wheel to be rotated to check for an out-of-round condition and allow the wheel to be trued is the first item. Clamping the wheel axle in a vise works as well for this as anything. (The wheel can be positioned vertically or horizontally, as long as it will turn freely.)

Some kind of indicator which can be fixed into position to check trueness will be needed. For the actual lacing, a spoke wrench or small adjustable wrench and a screwdriver are all that's needed. Once you have all the materials, and the rim and hub are clean and ready, decide on the pattern and if necessary make a rough sketch of the way it should look when completed. Take your time, get the spokes inserted into the hub and laid out in the approximate position they will lace up in, then slide the spoke ends into the rim and install the nipples finger-tight. It's easiest to thread up each group of spokes going in the same direction, then come back and start with the next bunch. Once you have all the spokes installed in the rim and hub, and the nipples on finger-tight, put the wheel on the truing jig. Use the screwdriver to tighten all the nipples until the ends of all the spokes are about $\frac{1}{32}$ inch from the flat end of the nipple. Then position the indicating device so that it just touches the outside of the rim and turn the wheel slowly to see where spokes have to be tightened to bring the rim into alignment. Work carefully, going over and over the spoke pattern until each spoke has a good firm tension and the wheel is completely round. After the wheel has been checked for roundness, place the indicator so that it touches the side of the rim and check for lateral runout. Once the job is completed, file off the protruding ends of the spokes inside the rim and replace the rubber liner or tape it. After you've done a couple of lacing jobs on your own, you'll probably be in great demand by your buddies who'll want you to do work on their machines.

Recent developments in cast-alloy wheels for motor-cycles may do away with the wire-spoked wheel altogether in the very near future. The new design (for motorcycles, racing cars had alloy wheels years ago) offers several ex-citing promises. As tires for road motorcycles become larger and disc brakes become more commonplace, the demand for strength in motorcycle wheels goes up. The new-style wheels offer high strength, rigidity, and much truer surfaces because they are machined. Another factor is the light weight of these wheels. Reducing the unsprung weight of a motorcycle is probably one of the best ways to improve handling and riding qualities. Every pound of un-sprung weight removed will make the bike that much easier to handle and also safer. Prototype installations on some road-racing bikes have resulted in weight savings of as much as 40 pounds. When you consider that the total weight of a bike such as this may be only 200 pounds or so, it's easy to see the advantages!

Another thing that the one-piece alloy wheel will make possible is the tubeless tire on motorcycles. Much of the advance in tire design of the last decade has been in tube-less tires. Motorcycling may benefit greatly from the use of some of this knowledge in motorcycle tire design.

A number of specialized tire/wheel combinations are used in various motorcycle sports. Most of them have no bearing on the average rider's choice of equipment for his bike, but they are interesting and should be mentioned briefly. One such limited-use tire is used by ice racers to get traction on frozen track surfaces. The ice racer is a hardy individual who starts his version of motorcycle racing when the weather forces everyone else to put their bikes away for the winter. Large-diameter tires are equipped with long steel spikes, as many as one hundred per tire. The spikes are bolted through the tread surface and provide excellent traction on the slick ice. Watching a group of racers hanging it out in a turn on solid ice at 80 mph is a hair-raising sight, and the possibility of being run over by those spiked tires makes this one of the most dangerous of all motorcycle sports.

For those dedicated racers who make the yearly trip to the Bonneville salt flats near Salt Lake City, Utah, to attempt world records for speed on motorcycles, tires are built that have no tread at all, just a thin covering of rubber barely ⅛-inch thick over the cord. Perfect roundness is the ticket on a high-speed tire; any little defect will show up strongly at 300 miles an hour. Tires for Bonneville competition are so specialized that only a few hundred are manufactured each year. A single set of tires may travel only a few miles over the salt in several years, and be good for many years to come.

Motorcycle drag racers have a specialized tire of their own also. The rear tire on these quick-accelerating bikes is without a tread pattern, getting the maximum amount of rubber on the ground for every last bit of traction. A soft compound is used and some of the tires have a very short life expectancy. A Top Fuel bike which is capable of covering the quarter mile with top-end speeds reaching 175 mph will shred one of these slicks in about three runs! The drag bikes produce so much horsepower that they literally smoke the tire, spinning it against the track surface almost the entire distance. Probably no other sight in motorcycle racing is as thrilling as watching a Top Fuel bike exploding away from the starting line, its rear section completely hidden in a cloud of white smoke that trails back until the bike is nearly to the finish line.

The newest single-purpose tire to make the motorcycle scene is an offshoot of the dunebuggy craze. A tire designed like the ones used by sand dragsters with large paddles sticking out to provide traction in pure sand is now available. It gives the bike the appearance of some kind of strange two-wheeled tractor, but it works!

One thing's for sure. There's a tire/wheel combination for just about every taste and every pocketbook. No matter what part of the motorcycle world you participate in, good equipment is available to increase your enjoyment of motorcycling, and tires and wheels play a big part in getting the most out of your bike.

# Hitting the Trail

There is a deception in motorcycle riding that afflicts all who straddle a self-powered two-wheeler. It's called riding over your head, and it can become very involved. Fortunately, the cure is only a matter of more and more miles of experience as a rider. The trail bike is a great place to get that experience.

While it is true that the ultimate winners in most desert and closed-course off-road events favor the expensive "specials," or machines with stronger engines in the 250-cc class, it is equally as true that on a given day a really good 100-cc trail-bike handler can eat everyone alive. The answer is simply that when all things are put together—bike performance and rider finesse—the very lightweight trail bike is a competitor of herculean proportions. A kind of giant-killer. Because of the extra challenge the trail bike offers, a number of first-rate riders stick with it against the bigger machines.

Honda started the whole ball game when they installed one of their small-displacement engines in a lightweight "motorcycle size" frame. For the first time the neophyte rider could straddle a full-size motorcycle and feel as though he actually did have some control. Furthermore, he could afford two or even three of these lightweights for the price of one competitive middle-size bike, which meant he could even take the family along. The idea caught on like wildfire.

There is some discussion as to what is and what isn't a trail bike. The best answer lies with the manufacturer. The entire idea behind trail bikes is two-wheel transportation capable of taking the rider into remote stretches of back country. That automatically separates the bike from a dirt machine. That is, it is not originally designed for racing, although as stated, many experts do use it for competition. But as pure transportation the trail bike is hard to beat.

Getting into remote areas of the country has long been reserved for horse riders and walking backpackers. Unfortunately, this is a restrictive situation; horses are expensive to keep or rent, and hiking takes a great amount of time. Some specially geared scooter-type vehicles were invented during the early 1950s for big-game hunters facing this problem, but they were both slow and often uncomfortable to ride, with small-diameter tires that made crossing downed timber anything but pleasant. While the first trail bikes may not have been designed for these treks into the deep wilderness, they have come to serve that purpose quite well.

Perhaps the original idea was just for a small, easy-to-ride motorcycle that anyone could enjoy traipsing around the neighboring woods or hills on. At least the early Honda advertisements would tend to support this viewpoint. But the picnic idea quickly led to use of the trail bike for more distant riding purposes. Now it is unusual to see any kind of recreational camping vehicle heading for the open country without one or two trail bikes attached. Part of the reason is that a trail bike is perfect for the beginning rider, and for women and children who traditionally have needed to learn motorcycle riding on something a little less exotic than a 650 Triumph.

There is really a narrow line between what is a trail bike and what is a dirt bike, since they are both used on the dirt. For the sake of desert competition events, the trail bike has a class all its own, and includes those motorcycles with a displacement of 125 cc's and under. The average person won't have this problem of definition, however, as the trail bike will also usually be equipped with special large-sprocket gearing for slow travel over very rough terrain. In a way, the average trail bike looks a bit more like a road machine, sometimes equipped with a headlight as well as full fenders and a protective skid plate below the engine. The trail bike doesn't look as brutish or as much a racing-only unit as the real dirt bike.

But don't think that a bike must be under 125 cc's to be used as a true trail bike. You can run any dirt bike, up through a 500, on most any area a trail bike will cover. The real distinction should be the type of trails you expect to cover. In the East and Midwest, where there are numerous paths through heavily wooded areas, practically any bike can be used, at times even a full-dress road machine. The important thing in this kind of country is to concentrate on pure dependability; you wouldn't want to venture far into the Maine woods and then have a mechanical breakdown force you to hike out.

Out West, it's a different matter entirely. The long reaches of rocky desert and extremely rough mountain trails mean that a degree of toughness must be engineered into any trail bike used. The possibility of falling on a steep trail is almost a certainty, and you want a motorcycle that can take this kind of physical pounding without failure. Because of this wide difference in the requirement of ultimate strength, you will see more "production" trail bikes in the less mountainous East, while out West the tendency is to modify and refine the trail bike with special accessories designed to make it more dependable and more powerful.

Those trail bikes used in heavy timber country, in both the East and Northwest, will tend to be of lighter total weight than bikes for open country. The reason is simple:

Two types of road bikes, a Honda 4 at left with fairing and most of the equipment common to road racing, a Harley-Davidson chopper at right with extended "plunger" forks.

Nearly any kind of bike can be customized, even the lightweight English imports. Biggest distinguishing factor of custom is the front fork.

This three-wheel "trike" was built for singer Sammy Davis, Jr., is kept at the Reno, Nevada, museum run by casino owner Harrah.

*All photos Street Chopper*

Small Triumph English bike has long custom tubing front fork with spring under compression for suspension, frame is "raked" to get chopper appearance rather than cutting and "raking" the neck to keep frame level. The more a neck is raked the harder the bike will be to steer.

Customizing must take in the entire bike to win show trophies. Note how frame has been molded behind rear wheel adjustment.

A great deal of molding with fiberglass is necessary to smooth off undersides of most bike gas tanks and area around neck.

Rear fender of this Harley-Davidson has been molded to the rigid frame; exotic paint job is extremely eye-catching on the street.

Harley-Davidson Sportster engine has transmission case integral with crankcase, the easy way to tell Sportster from the larger H-D 74. American V-twin design is not silk-smooth but it is powerful and dependable.

Vertical single and twin designs are common on English imports, may or may not have transmission integral with engine. These bikes remain popular today with off-roaders who want power but light weight in 4-stroke engines.

*Both photos Street Chopper*

The motorcycle must receive home care if it is to last. Learning to adjust chain properly is covered in every manual.

ABOVE: It is very easy to bend a wheel in tough off-road conditions, or even by hitting chuck-holes in the highway. Some rims can be straightened at home.

RIGHT: Eye-balling a rear wheel as it is turned will show if spokes need adjusting to true the wheel.

Front brake hub cover has worn shaft, should be replaced. Most bike parts are inexpensive, especially on lightweights, but to keep riding cost down the owner should do as much of his own work as possible.

*Cycle Guide*

BOTTOM OPPOSITE PAGE: Most bike engines are ruined in off-road use by faulty intake system air filtering. Filters must be checked and cleaned after every off-road ride, all intake system fittings checked to see that they seal properly.

Special speed equipment is available for practically every motorcycle sold in America, including auxiliary superchargers with Gilmer-belt drive like this one shown.

*Cycle Guide*

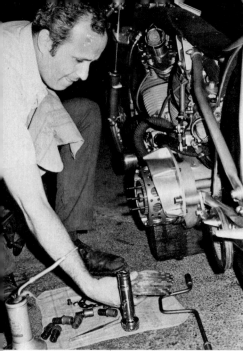

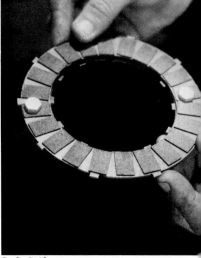

RIGHT: Clutch disc has bonded facings that can, and do, wear out. Some clutches run in oil for cooling, others are dry.

LEFT: The home mechanic can definitely repair a clutch, and it can be done in a short time. Any time the clutch is slipped excessively, heat build-up will cause short clutch plate/disc life.

Primary chain life is good on most bikes; clutch housing usually doesn't give much trouble. If possible, never disassemble a bike without shop manual.

A degree wheel bolted to crankshaft tells mechanic exactly where pistons are relative to valves for perfect valve timing, imperative for hop-up artist using special racing camshafts.

Points, condensers, and magnetos are most troublesome spots on most bikes. Learn this area of your machine well, especially before going off-road.

LEFT: Tillotson carburetor as used on Harley-Davidson motorcycles. Most carburetors are small, uncomplicated; their worst enemies are vibration and dirt. RIGHT: Front forks must do terrific duty even under road conditions, off-road they take terrible punishment. Special forks are available for competition, but they are not inexpensive. Springs are inside tubes.

Honda 350 vertical twin is good dual-purpose road and competition bike.

Honda 125 is excellent for beginners who have not ridden motorcycle before. Some experts get outstanding off-road performance from this size in races.

*All photos Cycle Guide*

Honda 250, still the lightweight chassis but with a slightly more powerful engine. Do not buy too small a bike at beginning.

Very popular road machine is Honda 350 Four. Also in 4-cylinder line-up are 500- and 750-cc versions.

*All photos Cycle Guide*

Husqvarna is considered one of finest off-road and competition bikes available; stress is on dependability and craftsmanship.

Bultaco is low-silhouette job that can be used for highway use as well as off-roading.

The Harley-Davidson Sprint is small-displacement bike imported to compete with rash of lightweights.

Harley Sportster remains one of most popular medium-weight road bikes ever built. Even used Sportsters have high resale.

*All photos this page Cycle Guide*

Full dresser Harley 74 is great for cross-country highway riding, but too heavy for good off-road use.

Small engines adapted to bicycle-like frames are not motorcycles, but they are common low-cost transportation in foreign nations.

Sidecars are becoming more common in U.S.; they have been mainstay of family motorcycling in Europe for decades.

*Cycle Guide*

In size the midi-cycle is somewhere between the mini-bike and lightweight motorcycle; they are ideally suited for youngsters learning how to ride. Many closed-course race tracks have classes for novice riders on midi-cycles.

The true mini-bike has small displacement 2- or 4-stroke engine, small wheels, and basic tubing frame as shown. These are not legal on the street unless equipped with full lighting and licensed.

you often have to horse a motorcycle over fallen timber and the heavier the motorcycle the more difficult a ride becomes. Yet this problem of weight is a paradox, because timber is usually associated with higher mountains. In the West, where trails commonly top an altitude of 10,000 feet, the very small engines (under 100 cc) often do not have enough performance at higher altitudes for even mediocre work. Thus the western mountain trail bike must be lightweight, but it must also have an abundance of horsepower. While all this power will not usually be used at the lower elevations, when the rider is at a high point on the trail he will end up with roughly the same amount of power that a stock engine would produce at sea level.

All this really means is that sooner or later the trail-bike owner is going to start custom-tailoring his particular motorcycle to his type of riding. The older couple who just putter around the lakeshore can get by with the Honda 50, but that little machine won't even begin to do the job for a hunter who decides to ride the Sawtooth Mountains of central Idaho. It is wisdom, therefore, to do some planning before purchasing that initial trail bike.

As a rule, the average young boy will find it no trouble to learn how to ride a trail bike of as much as 250 cc's, especially if the bike is geared to give good low-speed operation. The same bike fixed up as an off-road racer would be far too difficult to master as a first attempt. An adult male will not have much trouble with any bike, even those of 500 or more cc displacement, again if the gearing is low. Nothing will so discourage a rider as a highly modified dirt machine that does not run well below 50 mph!

Young girls and older women should never learn to ride on a large motorcycle. Usually the larger displacement bikes are heavier, which automatically makes them difficult to control for a woman, and the female is not accustomed to strong engine response. Therefore a happy medium might be a 125-cc or smaller bike for the female, a 175 for the male. The adult woman can rapidly learn how to handle a trail bike, and handle it extremely well, but she will seldom wish to progress to any motorcycle above 250 cc.

The young boy or man who plans on using his trail bike exclusively for sports riding—around town, occasionally off-road—will usually start with at least 175 cc. Experience shows that as he becomes acquainted with his riding abilities, he will begin "trading up" to larger and more powerful machines, until he often ends up in the 350-cc class. But if the person really does use his bike for trail riding, he will tend to keep the 175 longer and very seldom purchase anything over 250 cc. If he goes into some form of competition, there is no limit to what he might do. As already mentioned, he might stay with the 125-and-below "trail-bike" racing class and do very well. Or he might continue right on through dirt bikes to professional road racing. Whatever happens, the competition-oriented rider will be the first to admit that one particular type of bike, or one specific make, will seldom be around his garage more than two years in a row. Because of fantastic improvements in all facets of performance, the competitive rider must continue to improve his mount or forget the high incidence of winning he would like.

Learning to ride a trail bike is almost exclusively a matter of practice. Fortunately, there is a method of practice that precludes use of the motorcycle, a method widely used by young boys. A mini-bike, or even a bicycle with small-diameter tires (the "Stingray," etc.), makes an excellent platform on which a fledgling rider can try his wings. The idea is to ride the mini-bike or regular bicycle over rough terrain, especially some hilly areas, where the rider may at times have to jump off the vehicle to keep from falling. This would be the case in trying to go around the edge of a steep incline. Having learned how to dismount well, and how to use body weight, the new rider will be able to use a trail bike to much better advantage initially. At first, ride the trail bike over the very same area used with the mini-bike or bicycle, which will give confidence that the two types of vehicles respond to shifts of body weight in the same way, and then progress to more difficult country. In any case, do not buy a new trail bike and immediately head for the wilderness zone.

Generally, the lighter the weight of the trail bike, the easier it is to learn how to ride. When the bike is geared to run slowly and smoothly, it is possible to keep the engine running at a high-enough rpm so it will not bog, and the new rider can practice slow-speed balance and weight shifting. It is practically impossible to learn well on a bike where the engine bogs and runs erractically at this slow speed. As the rider's talent improves, so should his willingness to try new tests. But beware the first rule of motorcycle riding: When you think you are getting good, you will take a hard fall. And a fall from a slow speed can be just as injurious as one from racing speed. For this reason, always wear full riding clothing at all times.

If you use nothing else, always wear a helmet! This cannot be stressed enough. Too often, the new rider will spend several hundred dollars on a motorcycle and will neglect to spend $25 on the helmet that might save his life. There is a great variety of motorcycle helmets available today, ranging in price from the poor "cheapies" to those recommended for all-out competition. Do not buy a cheaply made helmet. The best guide you have is to purchase a helmet that meets the safety regulations established by your local state Department of Motor Vehicles, or by SEMA (Specialty Equipment Manufacturers' Association). Any helmet that meets these standards will have that information firmly affixed, and the motorcycle accessory dealer will make you fully aware of the requirements.

Should you experience a difficult fall and the helmet is banged up, take it in so the dealer can inspect it. Often a helmet will suffer bad damage from what would seem an insignificant fall. If it has a bad spot caused by an accident, helmet strength can be impaired critically, so that the next time you need it, the helmet might not be strong enough.

Use a helmet face shield or goggles that are approved by the motorcycle shop and are unbreakable. Check motorcycle racing gloves and you'll note padding on the glove backside. This is used for a reason, and one trip over the handlebars will be demonstration enough. Were you to go racing, you'd want a full set of "leathers," a leather jacket and pants that would save your own skin if you unloaded. The average trail rider isn't going so fast, however, so good Levi jackets and pants seem the most popular. Extra attention must be paid to boots.

The casual trail biker might be tempted to ride in everyday shoes, or even tennis shoes. Don't do it! Wear a boot that comes over the ankle, yet is flexible (ski boots and footwear that is very stiff should be ruled out). It is not uncommon to have the foot slip from a footpeg and slap off a rock or tree trunk, and sometimes the toes can be pulled back beneath a peg by brush. Strong, protective footwear is essential. The hunter who uses a trail bike will already have the kind of boots necessary. Under no conditions should a trail bike (or any motorcycle, for that matter) be ridden barefooted!

Those trail bikes currently sold in the United States and intended for honest trail use will often include the "extras" that reduce the chances of walking out. The experienced biker will want to equip his machine with extra throttle and clutch cables, routing them alongside the operational cables. Then if a cable breaks, he has another. A section of good fuel line is often taped to the frame, as well as a new spark plug and spark-plug wire. An emergency tool kit should be kept somewhere on the bike, and include pliers, screwdriver, piece of sandpaper, short length of bailing wire, electrical tape, and so on. Even a little piece of ordinary hand soap comes in handy. Should the gas tank be punctured in a fall, moisten the soap and plug the hole. It works. But most important of all, carry four or five extra chain master links. The chain can, and will, come off. A few master links make repair a snap; without them, you walk.

Finally, always equip the trail bike with a U. S. Forest Service approved spark arrestor. You can be fined for operating a motor vehicle in the National Forests without such an arrestor (a spark from the exhaust pipe can start a serious forest fire), and the cost for one is low. Some production trail bikes even come with an approved arrestor already in place.

If you're going to ride on private land, it is wise to get the owner's permission, preferably written, and be aware of the harm a trail-bike tire can do to the trail. Do not break the rear tire loose just for the thrill of throwing a rooster-tail of dirt. This digs up the trail and invites premature erosion. Use just enough power to get where you are going, and gear down to reduce the chances of breaking loose. At the same time, be cognizant of noise. The great thrill of our wilderness is the lack of noise, at least man-made noise. When you get there, shut down. You'll make friends with everyone, and next year you'll be welcome again. After all, that's why you bought the trail bike in the first place.

# Dirt Bikes

While the trail bike might honestly be confused with the
more sophisticated dirt bike, one ride on the latter and
any confusion rapidly disappears. Essentially, the trail
bike is restricted to the lightweights, or the motorcycles
with engines in the 125-cc and smaller category. The dirt-
bike range is basically from 250 through 450 cc's, although
some 175s easily qualify as pure dirters, and only a couple
of brand names go over 400 cubic centimeters. Dirt bikes
are mainly highly refined middlweight motorcycles.

Since the middleweight classification is such a popular
sales area, practically every motorcycle manufacturer has
a strong contingent in the field. Further, nearly every
builder is active in evolution and improvement of his particular product through the various types of dirt competition scheduled by organizations around the world. There
are four types of off-road riding usually associated with

the dirt bike; trials (extremely popular in England and coming on strong in the eastern portion of the United States), motocross (very popular in Europe as a closed-course event and now big in America), the desert (meaning the scrambles, hare-and-hound, or enduro events that need plenty of wide-open spaces), and pure off-road recreation. Far and away the largest segment of dirt-bike users are the putters, riders who like to get away and ride in solitude, using the absolute concentration necessary for off-road touring as a kind of escape from everyday activities. But while this type of noncompetitive riding appeals to the older rider, young riders prefer competition.

The type of dirt bike selected will depend almost entirely on the type of competition envisioned, although it is possible to enter all forms of racing with minor adjustments to a well-balanced machine. But to be really competitive, the rider must become a super handler, or several different motorcycles will be necessary. Since the locality will have a great deal to do with the type of competition available, the decision may not be too hard. In the arid Southwest, desert racing is all the rage, with motocross an interesting sideline. In the East, where open territory is more difficult to find, the motocross and trials events are far better suited.

The trials events are usually low-speed affairs that stress maximum driver control in extremely difficult terrain. The object is generally to complete the course rapidly, but without touching the ground with a foot. It might seem simple, but the courses are laid out to cover swamps, mudholes, steep banks, downed timber, sand washes—anything designed to stall the bike. Trials are especially good for the beginning rider, since he can easily tell how his skill is improving. Since there is no great element of risk involved, trials can become something of a family activity. Trials are invariably muddy affairs, however, so be prepared to clean the bike thoroughly after each event.

Motocross is really nothing but an all-out race over a closed course that is generally situated to include hills, mudholes, tight turns, long sweeping high-speed turns, and jumps. Because the motocross course can be laid out in a small area, it can be a financial success for a promoter. Spectators can be accommodated in relative comfort, much of a track can be seen from a single vantage point, the course length and number of laps are restricted to give variety to the program, and riders of all degrees of skill can participate. Since motocross does hold a big appeal for both rider and spectator, the motorcycle companies spend large sums of money annually sponsoring factory individual riders and teams.

The better motocross tracks are on broken ground, usually the type of terrain considered poor for either construction or agriculture. Therefore the cost of creating a good track is not great, and the track may even be in the center of a community. Where the track is near or in town, muffler sound-level laws are strictly enforced by the promoter. This may reduce a bike's performance slightly, but all competitors will have the same handicap.

Since motocross is really a major form of racing, some-times with lap times similar to hard-surface road racing, it is necessary for the novice to attain a high degree of riding skill before he can hope to be really competitive. But this is very possible, since most motocross tracks are open to the public throughout the week at a nominal charge. The best advice to anyone wanting to learn moto-cross racing is simply to watch the experts. Observe how they approach and negotiate each and every section of the track, then develop similar skills at reduced speeds. Only practice will bring improvement. Quite often, a superior rider on an inferior bike will run away from the pack. Once you've decided what you think a good rider is doing, ap-proach him and ask for pointers. Most riders are more than willing to help, but they prefer this sort of question during the week rather than on race day.

While trials encourage the selection of good clothing, such clothing is essential to motocross work. Helmet, gog-gles, gloves, good boots, and protective trousers and jackets are all necessary. You must assume that you are going to fall on the motocross course; even the best professional do. The secret to winning is how rapidly you can get under way again.

Trying to be fancy is not necessarily the ingredient for winning, either. Some of the very best professionals will pull the front wheel often on a course, riding the rear wheel only (especially in mud and water sections). This one-wheel act does serve a purpose (it gets the engine up out of the mud or water). But sometimes it is more a stunt than smart riding. When the competition is really tough, the experts will never be seen stunting.

Body english is, however, very much a part of motocross riding, and this is where some early training in trials comes in. The trials events teach superb balance, and this very same balance can be applied to the motocross track, only at much greater speeds. The expert motocrosser will often be setting up for the next section of track while the bike is in the air at a jump. Perhaps he will enter the jump with the motorcycle sideways, so that when he lands he will be in a slide but heading straight down the course. Sometimes he might even change the "shape" of the bike in midair by throwing his body weight a certain way. It is all truly fascinating to watch, and exhilarating to master.

To be a good motocross rider does not mean you will automatically be an expert on the desert, however. And neither is the reverse necessarily true. Open-country racing is a different type of riding, and it normally requires endurance and concentration far in excess of that needed for short closed courses. Desert races may vary in length from the short 10- and 15-milers to the enduros of 100 and 200 miles to the ultimate races such as the Mint 400 and the Baja 1,000. On the desert the rider must find his way by following markers (lime, strips of cloth tied to bushes, and so on), learn to read the terrain (10-foot-deep gullies appear seemingly from nowhere), go very fast, and be able to repair his bike if it conks out 100 miles from nowhere.

Desert racing has been the grandaddy of American off-road motorcycle activity, but by its very nature it has been restricted to the arid Southwest. In the early days when there was little else to ride, the heavyweight bike was supreme, but the coming of the light-heavies (Triumph, BSA, etc.) ended the Harley domination, and in turn the big Limey bikes have been put out by the middleweights. In open-country racing, power must be abundant yet the chassis must be extremely rugged and flexible as well as light enough to allow rider control in all situations. Whereas the motocross course will have a number of well-known built-in hazards, the open-country course will be practically unknown. Straying from the established course even a few feet to either side may mean an unscheduled cruise off a cliff or into a deep ravine. Yet to be competitive, the desert rider must go at maximum pace every moment.

Some of the shorter races of 50 or 60 miles will include three or four laps of a 15- or 20-mile course. The first time through is usually one of navigation, but after the markers have been torn or blown away, memory must serve for guidance. Since the lap courses pass the starting line several times (usually, but not necessarily), it is possible to ride the course and make needed repairs during the race at a pit stop. Not so the extended races such as the Baja 1,000.

The Baja race is really not 1,000 miles, but it is very close to it, and the punishment is fantastic. Generally two riders take the course, each for half the distance. In the early races it was most common to see the motorcycle entries literally vibrate apart. The manufacturers took note of the weak point in design or production, and the result has been a far better breed of off-road bike from the experience.

Preparation of the dirt bike will follow that of the trail machine, although the racing dirt bike (and perhaps even the bike used for leisure desert riding will include all the safety and emergency equipment (spare cables, spare chain links, tape, and so on) in addition to special options. These might include different front forks with greater length and consequent travel for the rough terrain, with the head angle increased slightly, as it is normally easier to ride at high speeds over rough ground with more fork rake; different rear springs and shocks; perhaps even a completely different frame.

The engine of a desert bike will usually be hopped-up, but the secret is in getting flexible (usable) power throughout the anticipated speed range, rather than brute power at maximum rpm's. Much attention must be paid to good lubrication, and maximum air flow that is never dirty. Highly specialized air and fuel filters have been developed for off-road use, and they are to be recommended always. Here's where a roll of freezer tape will come in handy. When a clamp vibrates loose and is lost, or a filter hose breaks, you can use the tape to make an emergency repair that will save the engine from extensive dust abuse.

To be really competitive in the longer off-road, desert

events such as the Mint 400 or Baja 1,000, extra attention must be paid to possible failure from vibration. Gas tank fractures, frame splits, possible tire puncture—all these things must be planned for and the rider must be capable of making repairs with a minimal number of tools or spares. This is really where experience pays off in off-road racing.

The longer races also require extensive mental preparation by the rider. It is usually necessary to scout the intended course two or three times in advance, making route maps that can be unrolled during the race. In the Baja races (there is a Baja 500 as well as the longer event), there are few road signs, and those are poorly placed. Hard-surfaced roads make up only about 10 percent of the course, and the remainder is either seashore sand or brutal volcanic rocks. The Mint 400 has been different through the years, but almost always there is a segment that runs through hub-deep southern Nevada talcum dust that is murder on bike and rider. Finding the way in the Mint is easier, but the riding is no less difficult.

While the majority of desert races are restricted to the Southwest, there is perhaps much more off-road racing taking place in the more inhabited areas of the country. In the heavily wooded mountains of the far Northwest, bike enthusiasts use forest trails for a combination motocross, trials, and enduro contest that is really rugged. In the eastern part of the nation some extended off-road racing is possible, although the closed short course is more common. The objective is to get experience wherever it is available, and then branch out to other forms of off-road riding as the opportunity arises.

Trying to keep abreast of what is happening in the off-road scene is often difficult unless you live in the hot spots, such as Southern California. There are a number of motorcycle weekly newspapers available, usually sold at bike shops, with a full list of forthcoming activities. Always telephone ahead to a distant activity, however, to check on any last-minute scheduling changes. Once you get around to a number of different events, the sponsors of those activities will add your name to their mailing lists for direct contact.

The very best way to become involved in any form of off-road riding is still the motorcycle club. Nearly every area where there is organized riding will have one or more clubs that specialize in this form of competition. The advantages of club membership are ready access to assistance at the events (in the form of a pit crew) and a group of experienced riders who will take extra effort to teach the novice better techniques of riding. Club members also often get discount tickets on parts from local bike shops.

As experience is gained in off-road riding, whether in competition or just for leisure, the enthusiast will usually work up the scale in motorcycle power. Where he might start with a 250 that at first seems far more powerful than he can ever master, within a few weeks his ability will have progressed to where a 350 is more to his liking. The obvious conclusion might be that purchase of a big-horsepower

450 would be better right from the start. This is sometimes the case, but usually the novice rider will not master the bigger machine completely, and his confidence will never be as great as it would be if he had worked up through the bike sizes.

Often the progressive motorcycle dealer will work out a trade-in agreement in advance of your first dirt-bike purchase, wherein he agrees to accept the bike back when you're ready to trade up in engine size. This is perhaps the most economical route to take, staying with one brand of motorcycle until you've found the size bike you can most comfortably ride. While it might seem best to get the most powerful motorcycle available for your class of riding, the really good riders have proven time and again that you can go quicker when you have complete command of the bike. That means that perhaps you may be able to ride a high-horsepower machine, but on it finish tenth or twentieth, while on a lighter bike you might place first or second.

Finally, the only way you'll ever find out about dirt bikes is to participate. Whether this is on a vacant lot, the Mojave Desert, or the local motocross track doesn't matter. Just get out and do it.

# For Street Use Only

Power to burn! That defines the current crop of large motorcycles designed for highway use only. Unlike the touring bikes of a generation ago, when comfort and reliability were considered more important than sheer acceleration, today's machines are being produced with power to weight ratios that would have seemed at home only on the race track a few years ago. To be sure, there are still bikes like the Harley 74 and the BMW 750 which are designed from the ground up to give a smooth ride over long distances. They have good brakes, excellent carrying capacity, and rank as the premium large road motorcycles of all time for touring.

But the bikes that have captured the public's imagination are the Honda 750 and Kawasaki 500. Both of these bikes will cover a quarter mile from a standing start in less than 13 seconds. The Kawasaki 750, new bigger brother to the 500, will get there in less than 12 seconds! Three- and four-cylinder machines, directly descended from the championship road-racing bikes built by these companies, are springing up like weeds, offering the prospect of neck-snapping performance for just about every pocketbook.

Both of the major English manufacturers offer 750-cc three-cylinder machines that will go over 125 mph, and similar performance is provided by the Norton 750 Twin, which somehow manages to pull a considerable amount of power from its two cylinders. On the home front, the Harley-Davidson Sportster, a growling brute of a bike, has been increased in displacement from 55 to 61 cubic inches, giving it the best power to weight ratio of the three road bikes produced by the only American builder of motorcycles.

Along with increased engine performance has come better handling and braking. With only a few exceptions, the new "muscle bikes" sport a disc brake on the front wheel, and new chassis design allows higher speeds in comparative safety. Today's rider can walk into the showroom of almost any brand and ride out on a bike whose performance is that of out-and-out racing bikes only a couple of years ago.

How did this surge toward high-performance street machines get started? Americans have always been interested in making things go faster or higher or quicker or deeper. It's part of our nature. As motorcycle road racing became a more popular spectator sport in the 1960s, the desire to have a more powerful street bike became stronger. Racing does improve the breed. When the manufacturers in Japan and Europe discovered this active interest on the part of the American rider, it was only a matter of time until horsepower ratings started upward, and weight went down. The biggest surprise to me is that it was so long in coming. The most admired American motorcycle had for years been the Sportster, a hunk of iron that has the stump-pulling power of a tractor, and a healthy exhaust note that seems to hypnotize onlookers with a sound of power like an expensive racing car. The only drawback to the high-performance Sportster (there are two basic models, one with electric starting, the other which is the performance model has a kickstart and a tiny gas tank that only holds a couple of gallons of gas) was the fact that the small gas capacity only allowed about 60 miles of travel before the rider had to stop to fill up. A lot of veteran riders were amused at the television series "Bronson" in which the hero rode all over North America without filling the tank.

The import superbikes have performance to match and in some cases pass the American Harley Sportster, but it's become a symbol of the big-bike movement, and despite a pricetag several hundred dollars higher than the imports, Harley manages to sell every one built each year. As a matter of fact, the Sportster image is so strong with the young affluent buyer that Harley has recently introduced a stripped-down version of the 74 called the "Super

Glide." This bike has the larger 74-cubic-inch displacement engine, but comes equipped with Sportster front forks and a patriotic paint job. It's quite a handful for the average rider, with lots of power and a front brake designed for a much lighter machine.

Even the staid European bike makers are starting to get in on the act. At a recent manufacturers show, Moto Guzzi displayed a new sport model of their 750-cc twin. This is an interesting bike. All the Moto Guzzi engines are V-twins, but unlike the Harleys which are arranged fore and aft so that the engine is inside the frame, the Moto Guzzi engine sits sideways in the frame with the heads sticking out on each side. It is very similar to the BMW which has twin opposed cylinders that stick out flat from the sides of the frame. BMW also has its lightened and sporterized version for the rider who feels that sheer performance is more important than the traditional BMW emphasis on riding qualities and a quiet engine.

What's it like to ride one of these big machines? They can be a handful of troubles for the inexperienced rider. All are capable of speeds in excess of 100 miles an hour, and several will do over 125 in stock trim. The two-stroke contingent, represented by the Kawasaki and Suzuki and Yamaha, have the fastest accelerating bikes. The Kawasaki Mach III, the first import to be specifically designed for street use as a sprinter, will reel off speeds and elapsed times for the standing quarter mile which will delight any drag-racing fan. It's a tough bike to ride, since you can lift the front wheel simply by twisting the throttle. It suffers from poor weight balance to further accent this tendency to wheel stand, and early production models had a swing-arm flex problem which caused them to handle badly in corners at high speed. Despite the handicaps mentioned, it is a thrilling bike to ride once the novice gets over the fear of the quick, pipey burst of top-end power. It is one of the lightest of the superbikes, weighing only a shade over 400 pounds with a horsepower output of 60 or better. From a standing start, it doesn't feel nearly as strong as the Harley Sportster or similar low-rpm engines, but the power comes on suddenly above 5,000 rpm, resulting in the lifting of the front wheel if the rider doesn't react quickly.

The recently introduced big brother of the Mach III, a 750-cc version called the Mach IIII, has more power but delivers it at a lower rpm and with a broader power band, making it much easier to ride. The potential of the Mach IIII is higher, and it will cut a quick quarter mile in less than 12 seconds.

The quickest of the four-stroke bikes is the famous Honda Four, a four-cylinder 750-cc machine. It has probably the most advanced four-stroke powerplant yet introduced to the general public. Although by some standards it's a heavyweight bike at 520 pounds, the Four is capable of running with the lighter Kawasaki, and has amassed a considerable number of records at drag strips across the nation. It is also one of the most popular bikes to hop-up, with a vast amount of speed equipment available to the owner who wishes even more power. Like the Kawasaki, it has a brother, the 500 Four, somewhat milder, but still big enough to rate in the big-bike category. (Both companies have introduced multi-cylinder bikes even smaller than 500 cc, but their performance leaves them out of the super-bike class.) The Honda Four is a delight to ride, one of the best I've handled on the open road. It can be taken deeply into the corners, braked, then accelerated smartly out and onto the straight. I know of one fellow who bought one in L.A. and left that same day for New York. He said the bike gave him no trouble at all on the trip; the only problem was, several cars almost ran him off the road trying to get a look at the bike!

Back in the mid-fifties a group of riders who favored the big stripped-down Harley-Davidson 74s got quite a bit of publicity as motorcycle gang members. Probably the most prominent of these "gangs" was the Hell's Angels. They were supposed to be everything bad about motorcycling wrapped up in a set of dirty Levi's, and quickly earned the nickname one-percenters, meaning they were supposed to be one percent of the total motorcycling public. The stripped-down and chromed bikes they rode became known as "choppers." Today, despite the fact that the major motorcycle organizations still prefer to ignore the chopper and chopper riders, they have become something like 10 to 15 percent of the street riding public.

While some of the chopper builders and riders still hang

on to the bad-guy image, the majority are simply enthusiasts of a rapidly growing sport of customizing and hopping
up large motorcycles. Dozens of motorcycle shows are held
in this country each year, and they draw large crowds of
spectators to see these beautifully painted and chromed
machines. In some areas they far outdraw the custom cars
and hot rods which have been on the show circuit for many
years.

Although many choppers have been built from Hondas
and Triumphs (and practically every other brand you can
name), to the purist a chopper is based on either the Harley 74 or the Sportster. Until the last four or five years,
anything else would have been looked on with condescen-
sion. Things have changed, and the reason for the change
was the explosion of the imported superbikes. One motorcycle writer who didn't think too much of the chopper and
its advocates once said that the chopper was nothing more
than mobile jewelry, not really suitable for riding. Nothing
could be further from the truth. As soon as other brands of
motorcycles with the kind of street performance that the
Harley-Davidson offered became available, the chopper
builders began to use them as the basis for new and exciting creations. It is now common to see choppers built from
Honda 750s, Kawasakis, and other import machines.

Starting with the basic bike, the chopper builder will
first strip everything off that does not fit the current pattern of styling, then usually the frame will be altered so
that it sits lower in the rear. The classic chopper is based

on a copy of the early rigid-rear-end frame. The front end is he next thing to be modified. The most obvious change on the chopped bike is the extended front forks. Normally the front portion of the frame is altered so that the extended forks don't raise the bike much higher off the ground, a process called "raking." It is this extending and raking of the front end that has caused the most comment from nonchopper motorcycle riders and law-enforcement officials. Many feel that it has an adverse effect of handling, and should be forbidden by law. Without trying to start a debate with other members of the motorcycle sport, I'll simply say that while extreme extensions and rakes will have a slight effect on low-speed handling, it gives the bike a considerable increase in straight-line stability out on the highway. Along with the frame and front-end alterations, the chopper builder will add a rear fender and back support known as a "sissybar." This little item became common because a law was passed in California requiring a handhold on each bike capable of carrying a passenger. Some of the wilder elements of the chopper sport decided that to have a handhold was a sissy style of riding for the passenger, and made tall, ornamented bars to show their disapproval. What started as a protest soon became the height of chopper style. Each sissybar is supposed to be the best place for the owner to demonstrate his individual taste, and some of the designs are quite impressive.

The other area of individual taste is paint. Each bike owner strives to outdo the others, and many exotic and

167

unusual paint jobs are seen in the shows and on street machines. Everything from flawless black lacquer to multi-hued metalflake can be found. It's not unusual to find that a chopper owner has invested as much as $500 or more just in the paint on his wild creation. Offset with lavish chrome, it is a sight that has to be seen to be believed. Underneath the paint, the frame is often molded into sculptured shapes with body putty. Added to this is an engine that will move the bike effortlessly down the highway at the maximum speed permissible by law. The total chopper is a machine designed by the rider just as the hot rod is designed by its owner to be a reflection of his personal taste, and to his requirements.

Whether chopper, stocker, or hopped-up street racer, all these big bikes have one thing in common. They all are designed for carrying the rider swiftly down the highway. Touring or cross-country riding is the part of the motorcycle sport which probably receives the least attention by the writers of the many motorcycle magazines. Unlike the noise and glamour of a racing event, the touring bike and its rider sort of fade into the surroundings. Nevertheless, it's the best way I can think of to see the country.

Practiced road riders who are making trips of long distances take along a variety of things to equip themselves to handle almost any situation. First comes a good set of tools and a few of the most commonly needed parts. A couple of master links for the drive chain, a spark plug or two, a tire-patching kit and pump, and a spare set of fuses for the electrical system. On a bike with saddlebags or other means of carrying fair-sized loads, the rider will throw in a couple of cans of oil, especially for two-stroke bikes, and a roll of electrical tape or wire. (I carry both, having been in the position of being broken down in some mighty empty spots over the years.)

For creature comforts, a bedroll and air mattress, plus a tube tent or shelter half, will fill most meeds. If you are touring over long distances where cooked food isn't available at the roadside, or are trying to save money, stop in at a store that handles backpackers equipment. They have a wonderful selection of freeze-dried and packaged foods that don't take up a lot of space. Cooking ware is up to the individual, but as far as I'm concerned, the army-style mess kit is the best. The backpackers supply will also have the best of the sleeping bags or bedrolls. Light in weight and small when wrapped, they are ideal for motorcycle use.

The right clothing depends on the area you will be traveling. In the summer months, only boots and a stout jacket for protection against accidental spills are really necessary (and, of course, a helmet and goggles or glasses). If you are heading into country that has a lot of rain, or are traveling in spring and fall, some kind of foul-weather raincoat or suit is a good idea. Several companies offer riding suits that are rainproof and quite comfortable. Spare clothing, which is usually a change of underwear and some socks, can be rolled up inside the bedroll, saving space. The real idea of seeing the country by motorcycle is to get down to the essentials of travel and I recommend doing with as little extra stuff as possible. It will not hurt to get along without some of life's little conveniences for a couple of weeks, and a lot of riders find that they enjoy themselves if they sort of rough it.

I try to plan my rides in advance so that at least every three or four days I can spend the night in a motel or a campground which has a shower and a facility for washing clothes. Other than that I don't stick to any sort of schedule. My personal equipment list is as follows: bedroll and tent, mess kit plus some dried foods, tools for minor repair, flashlight, one change of clothing, a fishing rod designed for backpackers which breaks down into several short lengths (I'm always pleased to have a fresh fish meal whenever I can get one), a good supply of maps, and enough cash to make sure I don't get caught flat-footed if the weather turns nasty and I have to take to a motel for a couple of days. Planning it this way means that I get maximum enjoyment out of a motorcycle trip because I'm prepared for all but the worst of calamities. I also leave a short list of where I'm expected to be more or less, so that if I don't turn up, they can get out a search party or something.

If possible, I prefer to tour with another rider. It's always nice to have a second pair of hands or a means of getting into town if something goes wrong that can't be fixed by the side of the road. Besides, after a day of riding, it's better to have someone to talk to while you're getting ready to hit the sack. There's a little bit of science to riding with a partner, especially if you are covering a lot of ground quickly. It's all right to ride side by side, but when moving fast, I prefer to ride single-file, so that each rider can use as much of the road as necessary. When riding single-file, leave a little space between bikes so that faster vehicles can get by you without having to pass both of you at the same time. This is even more necessary when riding at night. Drivers have a bad habit of misjudging the distance betwene themselves and a bikc, and my most interesting experience happened one late evening when a car tried to stuff itself between myself and a buddy when we were only a few feet apart!

In some ways, riding at night is safer than in the daytime. Your head- and taillights make the bike stand out much better at night to drivers ahead of you. I feel that the practice of burning the headlight in the daytime is a good idea. Just as in night riding, it gives the drivers of cars around you a better opportunity to see you before they start to change lanes or pass. Your biggest danger at night is not the cars, it's objects or animals in the road ahead. I have a good friend who clobbered a deer one evening on the mountain highway leading up to Big Bear Lake, California. He was pushing it a bit, trying to get into town before the temperature dropped below the comfort level, and was taking the corners with abandon. On one blind curve he suddenly found himself confronted by a small herd of deer that were crossing the road. The one that got him wasn't actually on the highway; it got confused and jumped in front of him from the roadside. He was pretty well banged up, and the deer and the bike were both writeoffs. The point of this is, don't just watch the road ahead of you in country where there may be animals roaming loose. You need to keep a close eye on the side of the road, because the sound of the bike and the light sometimes startles the animal and it will jump onto the road surface, leaving you the choice of hitting it or laying the bike down. That's when that hot, uncomfortable helmet and heavy jacket come in handy!

I once jumped on a bike that I had been doing some engine work on in the garage and started around the block for a midnight test ride. Since it was only going to be a short ride and I was so close to home, I didn't bother to put on a helmet or glasses. Down at the end of the block was a street light, and that's where I got into trouble. It was summertime, and the light had attracted a huge cloud of June bugs about the size of bumblebees. Boy, those things smart when you ride through them at about 50 miles an hour! I made a vow that evening never to ride anywhere without glasses or goggles and a helmet.

Learning to read the road conditions ahead is valuable to the road rider who is traveling over unfamiliar territory. Many of the highways leading into scenic spots and resorts require almost constant work to keep them in shape due to the terrific amount of traffic. Some of the signs of road work are: large gravel trucks coming from the direction you are heading, stored sand and construction equipment alongside the road, and the detour sign. Detours are dangerous for road bikes if they are graveled or dirt. Most bikes are a bit shaky on soft surfaces; their tires and suspension were not designed for it. If you must travel for any distance over rough ground on a touring bike, be careful. Just as dangerous, and probably more common, is the large patch of dirt and gravel left on the highway at the point where heavy equipment or logging trucks come on to the pavement. If you should come on one of these spots around a curve and are still leaned over for the corner, chances are you'll wind up in a ditch or worse. As was discussed in the chapter on wheels and tires, learn to read the terrain ahead of you like the off-road riders do. It'll save you some scraped skin someday.

Despite the warnings I've listed, riding a large, fast, road bike across the country on vacation is one of the most enjoyable and free-feeling things that a man can do. Unlike the car driver who is enclosed in a steel shell with glass sealing him off from the world around him, the bike rider gets very close to the sights, smells, and sounds of the countryside. Although you can now go from one coast to the other on modern, straight superhighways, the bike is much more suited to wandering down sideroads and following the old roads. With the few items of clothing and equipment that I mentioned, you're as free as a bird, only marginally dependent on civilization. Except for gas and oil,

the rider who wants to get away can literally ignore the
rest of the world for a month or more. It's a nice feeling,
restoring to a man's confidence.

The dream trip that I will someday make is to travel
from my home near Los Angeles to the Northwest, seeing
all of that area including British Columbia, then catch the
ocean-going ferry to Alaska. You have a number of choices
of landing sites in Alaska, and the trip is one of the most
exciting left in an area of rapidly encroaching cities and
superhighways. One of these days, I'm going to do it.
Maybe.

# Mini-Bikes Come in All Sizes

Not long after the Go-Kart became a national plaything, in the very late 1950s, Mini-Bikes screeched onto the scene in full force. Initially, these pint-sized motorcycles were home-bent versions of Kart construction, and performance was strictly a matter of backyard guts. You couldn't steer them, you couldn't stop them, and you couldn't ignore them. They were, and remain, great fun to ride, but at first they were just toys for the grownups. It wasn't until the mid-1960s that kids found just how enjoyable mini-bikes can really be. Manufacturers of "big" motorcycles were quick to capitalize on this market, especially our old friend Honda, and today there are mini-mini-bikes, mini-bikes, midi-bikes, and so on.

The term mini-bike applies to any two-wheeled motorcycle using an extremely short wheelbase (usually between 32 and 38 inches) and tires not over 14 inches in diameter. This immediately sets the mini-bike apart from the midi-bike, or mini-cycle as it has become known. Although both bikes may use the same engine, the mini-cycle will look very muhc like a three-quarter-scale version of a motorcycle, complete with spoke wheels, double-tube frame, and even road gear such as lighting, speedometer, etc. The basic mini-bike will be much smaller, usually with two-piece cast-alloy wheels and seldom with road accessories.

In the beginning, the mini-bike was introduced to karting as a kind of prank, a motorcycle-type plaything that could be built using kart parts. By the early 1960s, every kart track in the country was overrun by mini-bikes, and even the participants at more traditional automobile racing events found the litle machine useful for buzzing around the spacious track facilities. The bike was small enough to fit inside a car trunk, and in some cases even came to be a basic form of transportation for airplane owners. But it was, and remains, difficult to ride.

The extremely short wheelbase of a mini-bike, coupled with the low bike center of gravity relative to the higher rider center of gravity (which means that when a rider is astride, the total center of gravity is too hgh for good engineering principles) makes the bike prone to upend itself with little provocation. The earliest designs used the smaller kart motors, sometimes with only a mild 1½-hp four-cycle engine. With riding expertise came the inevitable search for increased power, and soon engines were doubling and tripling in power. Now it is possible to get a production mini-bike with a 15-hp motorcycle engine, a considerable package of performance that should be attempted only by someone with experience on less powerful mini-bikes.

The minis come in an assortment of sizes, the less powerful usually equipped with the shorter wheelbase, smaller tires, and generally less sophistication (solid front suspension, pull starter, and so forth). As the power increases, tire size will increase also, and things such as a kickstarter, highway accessories, etc., will be introduced. It is important to realize that tire size is directly related to how well a two-wheel vehicle handles; the larger the size the more stable will be the bike and the easier it will cover off-road conditions.

When shopping for a mini-bike, keep in mind that these machines are not intended as road bikes, although some indeed have lighting. The vehicle is so small that it is difficult to be seen in ordinary traffic conditions, and unless the bike is equipped with the more powerful engine, performance will be far inferior to regular traffic. The mini-bike, then, is essentially an off-road vehicle. As such, it can be an invaluable aid to learning the finesse of motorcycle riding.

Several years ago, at the height of karting activity, the editors of *Rod & Custom* magazine decided to sponsor the Tiny Bear run, a strictly-for-minis affair named after the famous desert/mountain motorcycle chase in Southern

California (Big Bear). It was anticipated that upwards of thirty or forty mini-bikes would show at the desert location. Instead, the crowd totaled closer to 300. Amazingly, only a very few youngsters were in the lineup, and the majority of older riders were veterans of larger machines. It turned out that practically every motorcycle rider had a mini-bike, if for no other reason than the challenge of learning how to ride it.

Because of the rash of traffic accidents caused by unlicensed mini-bikes used on city streets, most communities passed ordinances prohibiting the small bikes on streets unless the machine could be licensed (which meant headlights, good brakes), a move that effectively killed interest in the small machine during the late 1960s. Lately there has been a resurgence of interest as parents find the well-engineered mini-bike with a long wheelbase, large-diameter tires, full suspension, and an engine in the 5-hp range is ideally suited for training very young riders. It is now common to see mom and dad heading for the boondocks towing their trail-bike trailer, and tucked in there somewhere will be a mini-bike or two for the kids.

Coming on strong are the mini-cycles that really give a helping hand to the neophyte rider. Most kids are not big enough to handle a trail or dirt bike, simply because these machines are made for the average adult with long legs. However, if the same frame construction is scaled down slightly and smaller tires are used, a teenager can usually learn how to handle the same amount of horsepower.

Since mini-cycles are just one step removed from the regular-size motorcycle, they make ideal training machines for someone interested in some form of motorcycle competition. At the same time, they can easily be outfitted for legal street use and are large enough to be quite safe, although the majority of mini-cycles never see a paved surface. Costwise, the mini-cycle is about halfway between the mini-bike and a popular trail bike.

Many communities have now set up parks for use by mini-bike and mini-cycle enthusiasts, or at least have an area where the rider can practice his art without disturbing the peace and safety of others. Be advised that no rider should ever straddle such a machine as this until he has at least a good helmet, preferably some sort of boots, and a long-sleeved jacket. It is easier to have an accident on a small bike than on a larger one, and since the mini-bike is often capable of 60 mph, a seemingly simple accident can be serious.

Most good motorcycle shops will handle a reputable line of mini-bikes and mini-cycles, while at least one monthly magazine is devoted to the sport (*Mini-Cycle* combined with *Mini-Bike Guide*). Special riding resorts set aside for some form of motorcycle competition will often include competition for these smaller bikes, making this an ideal place to learn good riding techniques under controlled conditions.

Maintenance of the smaller motorcycles is extremely simple, with engines often no more complicated than for a lawnmower, and tires, chains, twist-grips, and similar paraphernalia available through most bicycle shops. As a training ground for the young enthusiast, the mini-bike can't be beat.

---

# Here Come the Choppers

The chopper is the hot rod of motorcycles. It comes in all colors, shapes, and sizes, and it may cost anywhere from $100 to $10,000. It is the glamour king of the sport.

Like the hot rod, the chopper has evolved from an ignominious beginning. Modified motorcycles have been a part of the sport since the very first two-wheeler hit the road, but these bikes were created more for competition than increased highway performance. The chopper was created for highway performance, quickly slipped into discredit, and during the last decade has suddenly loomed again as the custom segment of motorcycling.

As noted earlier, motorcycles are easily classified by ultimate use, although the majority are originally purchased as "dual-purpose" forms of transportation and recreation. The chopper, never intended for anything but highway riding and maximum rider comfort, becomes the luxury vehicle of the bike set. Special machines like the Harley-Davidson SuperGlide, which has the large 74-cubic-inch engine in the lighter-weight Sportster chassis, and the new large-displacement imports from Japan are beamed at the "sporty car" elements of motorcycling. Accessory performance equipment such as power add-ons for the engine, better brakes, personal handlebars and controls are part of the package. When all these things—road comfort, large engine, performance add-ons—are combined with a customized chassis, the result is pure chopper.

For years the term chopper has been synonymous with outlaw motorcycle clubs, with good reason. Immediately following World War II the used police and military-surplus motorcycle found a ready market with young men in need of scarce transportation. But like the car owners who were stripping fenders from Model A's, the bike enthusiasts were not content to have a stocker. Rear fenders were replaced by the smaller front fenders, bulky seats became small pads, everywhere possible the motorcycle was "chopped" to reduce weight (for slight extra performance) and to alter the appearance. Chopper owners naturally gravitated to one another and formed loose alliances that gradually became formal clubs and associations, and because of the obvious difference between their motorcycles and the common stockers, they were considered rather daring. In the beginning, hot rodders and chopper builders were held in the same regard—young men in greasy T-shirts and Levi's who were somehow slightly weird because they liked things mechanical. The coming of organization for hot rodding modified that image and gave the automotive enthusiast a direction for his hobby. The motorcycle enthusiast had no similar evolution.

Motorcycles remained something of an enigma on the American scene for two decades after World War II. Gradually, the outlaw clubs began to gain enough membership to warrant local attention, and when Marlon Brando flashed across the screen in *The Wild Ones,* everyone from Portland to Podunk knew what a chopper and an outlaw biker was. In the public image, the chopper was a stripped motorcycle (done because the bike was probably stolen) and an outlaw rider was just one step ahead of the law. The validity of these suppositions is open to debate, but in a way they have contributed mightily to the current popularity of customized motorcycles.

There is something very masculine about a motorcycle. It seems to say in every vibration that only a man can handle it, something like the stallion horse. Certainly only a person who understands and appreciates things mechanical comes to be an outstanding bike enthusiast, particularly the type who can build and ride the modified jobs. It is this masculine thing that has such great attraction to so many enthusiasts.

Where the chopper was once associated with the outlaw element, it is now the showcase of motorcycling. Few motorcycle dealers display their wares without at least one custom on the front row to draw attention. Some custom builders devote full time to making such show bikes for the trade. Greasy, stiff Levi's have given way to mod flairs and print shirts. The custom has become very much a part of what's happening in America.

As with hot rods, there are some definitive terms for choppers that probably only make sense to the serious enthusiast. Terms like rigid frame, straight leg, Frisco peg, and panhead all have significant meaning to the custom builder, but may be only vaguely familiar to the desert rider or road racer. Also as with hot rodding, the terms come and go as the chopper sport grows, and different sections of the country may have different names for specific items.

While Southern California tends to lead the nation in chopper activity, due largely to the year-round bike-riding weather, Northern California is considered the hotbed of innovation. What the Northern California builders are doing now, the country will be doing next year, so the claim goes. While this isn't entirely true, it is a fact that trends established in the Sacramento and San Francisco Bay area tend to become accepted building fashions elsewhere. Part of the reason may be the great number of custom motorcycle shows in Northern California during the rainy winter months. Whatever it is, no one disputes that Northern California choppers are among the finest built, as evidenced by the great number of Nor-Cal bikes appearing regularly in chopper magazines.

By comparison, bikes from more eastern areas tend to be less radical, sometimes due to restrictive state equipment laws, sometimes because of weather and road conditions. There are, however, a number of hot spots in chopper activity in the East and South. New Jersey, New York, Conecticut, and Massachusetts seem to be the leaders on the Atlantic seaboard, while Tennessee and Florida dominate the South. Bike for bike, these areas produce customs equal to those of California, but since there are so many more enthusiasts in the eastern half of the country the outstanding machines tend to be lost in the masses. But the sheer number of enthusiasts will tend to create a greater demand for premium workmanship in custom building, so that within five years the majority of outstanding choppers will probably be east of the Mississippi.

The term chopper does not limit the modified motorcycle to a pure custom in the traditional sense of the word custom. This term has come to mean any kind of machine that is dolled up in appearance only, with no performance The classic example would be the custom car and the hot rod. One was a lead sled, the other strictly for going strong. In bikes, chopper has come to mean any modified road motorcycle. It can be a Harley 74 with extended springer forks, rigid tail section and high-backed seat. Or it can be a Triumph Bonneville with Ceriani forks, plunger-shock tail section, low-rider seat, and a high-horsepower engine. The former is an adaptation of the show-only bike, while the latter leans heavily on the influence of drag-racing motorcycles. One is for comfort, the other is a street digger of the first order. In both cases, the machine has been altered visibly from the stocker.

Where just a few short years ago the chopper builder was forced to fabricate any and all custom parts, there is now a multimillion-dollar business tailored to meet his every need. Practically everything necessary to construct an entire chopper is available through hundreds of custom bike shops nationwide. In one case, A.E.E. Choppers of Placentia, California, sells a special Kit Bike that comes ready to paint and assemble. All you supply is the engine. A.E.E. Choppers is a good example of the fantastic growth in the chopper sport.

A number of years ago hot-rod owner acquaintance Tom McMullen came to me with the idea of marketing custom bike parts. In travels around the country, he had noted the number of custom bikes everywhere and was convinced there would be a buying public for special things like custom front forks and form-fitting seats. Following up on the idea, McMullen turned his hot-rod-building prowess to motorcycles, and within three years had created a company (AEE) acknowledged as the giant of the enitre motorcycle accessory industry with annual sales in the millions of dollars. Sales are for chopper parts only. There are now several dozen chopper parts manufacturers.

While there are some that claim only the rigid-frame Harley-Davidson 74 is a real chopper, the general consensus is that any modified bike becomes a chopper. Obviously this is a view shared by many, since the relatively new Honda 750 and 500 Fours are customized almost as often as the Harley 74 and Sportster. Given a few more years, and the fact that more Honda Fours are sold than Harleys, and chances are certain that the traditional chopper image may be considered only a sideways four-cylinder engine with individual exhaust pipes.

Since practically anything can be turned into a chopper, even the very small displacement two-strokes, the variety of styles is limitless. While most chopper builders tend to copy and improve upon some given style, there are enough pacesetters to keep fresh ideas flowing continually, a situation particularly advantageous to the low-buck type who wants to build it all at home.

Often the new chopper enthusiast will try to duplicate some chopper he has seen. This may or may not be the best approach. As a rule, the best finished product will result when the builder takes time to survey the field and then plan very carefully what he wants to construct. While it is great to see a chopper in living paint and chrome, it is not entirely necessary. Hours of pouring over the photographs in chopper-oriented magazines will give excellent ideas of what is, and what isn't, a good idea.

With a thorough knowledge of styling and general bike costs, decide on a realistic amount of money to be spent. With this guideline, select the type of motorcycle to be customized. The Sportster is a great chopper base, but

even a ten-year-old used Sportster brings premium dollars
on the used market. Not so common might be a Honda 450
or BSA, available at one third the Sportster price. Whatever you select, take into consideration the availability of
ready-made custom parts. The German BMW is a fine-
looking road machine, but there is practically nothing in
the line of custom parts made for it.

The only reason the Harley-Davidson has such a strong
following among traditional chopper enthusiasts is because
it was one of the original motorcycles to be customized by
Americans, along with the discontinued Indian. With a
rigid-tail-section frame and a contour seat, the Harley produces a very low appearance for the rider, quite unlike the
high perch common to the British and Japanese imports.
This distinct appearance, along with a high-torque engine
that will lug along smoothly in high gear, has made the
Harley the heads-on favorite for years. Because of this
popularity, the majority of all custom equipment has been
geared toward this make. All that is changing.

The Honda 750 is far and away the most popular high-
performance road bike on the market today, followed in
close order by the Harley Sportster (for the traditionalist),
and the Kawasaki and Suzuki three-cylinder two-strokes
(for the lightweight crowd, although neither is a lightweight). The big surge to large-displacement, super-fast
road machinery is a natural outgrowth of the motorcycle
boom, and a great boost for chopper fans.

Many lightweight bikes have been given the custom

routine, but because of the lack of bolt-on custom equipment, these bikes are usually owned by highly able mechanics. While it is possible to purchase special rigid frames for practically every engine of 500 cc's and over, there are very few rigid frames for smaller-displacement engines. When the demand becomes strong enough, as it surely will, such equipment for lightweights will be forthcoming. Also, specialist manufacturing companies will undoubtedly emerge to offer lower-demand articles. Already there are chopper firms that specialize in Japanese-only or British-only makes, so with lower overhead costs they will certainly begin serious work on the smaller bikes.

Selection of the bike for a future chopper, then, is not just a matter of working with what you have. While you may admire the Moto Guzzi, unless you're prepared to spend a lot of money at a customizer's shop, or unless you are a really good mechanic, you'll be better off to start with something for which there is an abundance of custom equipment. This isn't intended to discourage ingenuity, but experience has proven that the first-time attempt should be as uncomplicated as possible. Experience has also shown that the person who builds a really good "typical" chopper the first time will tend to create a really outstanding "different" bike on his second attempt.

When movie and TV actor Norm Grabowski started on his first Corvair-powered chopper, he knew there would be many bugs to work out, so he didn't go all-out on customizing the initial version. Instead, he concentrated on perfecting the mechanical details, both during construction and then in extended road testing. With this experience, and money gained from selling the first machine, Norm created a second Corvair chopper that was the envy of the entire sport. From first idea until the second machine became a reality was a long four years.

Too often, the new chopper enthusiast will begin a project with a limited conception of what a chopper really is. While magazines may show the average chopper as having a radically extended front end, a high-mounted peanut gas tank, and a super-low seat, the slinky low-rider is just as customized and just as much a chopper. Rather than be trapped into building something "like the other guy's," the wise builder looks at many different bikes and selects things from each he likes.

For example, there is a wide variety in front ends, and it is essential to be very careful when working in this area. There are two common front ends, the springer (a design used by most motorcycle companies until the early 1950s), and the telescopic "glide" (the modern collapsing tubular fork assembly). An early modification of the basic springer was the girder. This front end is basically very simple, and lends itself very well to smooth styling, but it lacks the essential quality of "trail factor," a special phenomenon peculiar to motorcycles that must be thoroughly understood by anyone working with customized bikes.

The most distinctive modification to a customized motorcycle is usually the front end, and too often builders

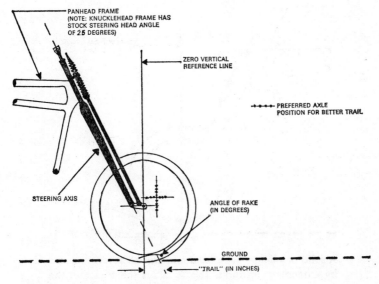

PANHEAD FRAME
(NOTE: KNUCKLEHEAD FRAME HAS
STOCK STEERING HEAD ANGLE
OF 25 DEGREES)

ZERO VERTICAL
REFERENCE LINE

PREFERRED AXLE
POSITION FOR BETTER TRAIL

STEERING AXIS

ANGLE OF RAKE
(IN DEGREES)

GROUND

"TRAIL" (IN INCHES)

Typical stock springer-type front end as used on early Harley
Davidson motorcycles. The "knucklehead" frame neck has 25 degrees rake (knucklehead refers to type of heads on H-D engine);
an increase in rake angle will further alter the already undesirable
caster problem of the front-end. Distance between vertical reference
line and steering axis line at the ground level is critical point when
figuring front end trail. (*Courtesy Street Chopper magazine*)

charge ahead with radical front-end changes without understanding the problems of front-fork modification.
Making a change just because someone else has made a
similar change does not mean the change is good. So consider modifications of the various types of front ends.

A stock front end can be extended any *practical* length
with or without raking the frame. That's a strong state-
ment, and obviously the catch is the word practical. It is

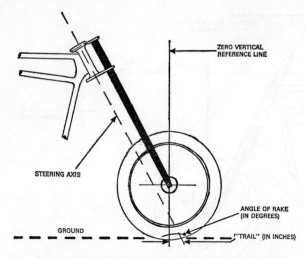

ZERO VERTICAL
REFERENCE LINE

STEERING AXIS

GROUND

ANGLE OF RAKE
(IN DEGREES)

!"TRAIL" (IN INCHES)

A solid or plunger-type front end can be severly altered by extending the forks. This so alters the trail that the front end caster is negligible and bike no longer steers well. (*Courtesy Street Chopper magazine*)

generally agreed among chopper builders that an 18-inch extension is certainly the very maximum, and that 8 inches seems to be practical with any of the glide-type forks. It is a common practice to install "slugs" when extending a glide front fork assembly. These are simply threaded extension pieces. They are not recommended. The safest method is to replace the upper slider tubes with new, longer chrome-moly steel tubing replacements of the desired length.

There is considerable controversy over the type of steel to use in modified motorcycle front ends. Some experts claim mild steel is plenty good, while others feel 4130

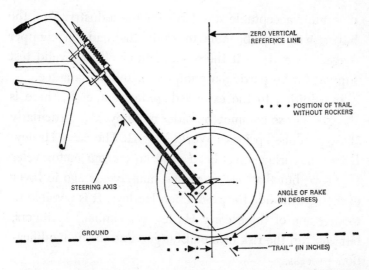

A custom springer with special longer "rockers" (tapered triangular pieces that connect axle to forks) will keep the trail factor within acceptable limits when rake (neck angle) is increased by frame work or extending forks. (*Courtesy Street Chopper magazine*)

chrome moly is the only answer. The truth rests solely with the buyer. Mild steel is not as strong as correctly used chrome moly, and in a front end subjected to high bending and twisting forces the mild steel will fail early. On the other hand, the molecular structure of chrome moly is such that incorrect welding will cause stress concentrations that may lead to early failure. In either case, a failure at 60 mph is a serious matter, so the buyer must be fully aware of his specific product. The better chopper accessory companies are currently putting various materials and construction techniques through a series of rigid tests to determine acceptable standards for the industry. You, the buyer, will then be able to study their ads in chopper magazines and see if the manufacturer offers a valid test support for his particular equipment, and a guarantee.

In addition to the extended glide front ends, there is the springer so common on older motorcycles, particularly those produced prior to World War II. The early Harley-Davidson springer has been used on custom motorcycles for years, but that design ceased many years ago in favor of the HydraGlide for production Harleys. It is possible to modify one of these early Harley (or similar) springers, but you run the risk of metal fatigue due to the modification process.

The girder front end is similar to the springer, in that both have coil springs to absorb road shock. These springs are usually mounted adjacent to the frame neck, but while the springer uses a special front axle "rocker," the girder does not. In the springer design, the main fork assembly is rigid with the frame and the spring action is caused by a secondary fork ahead of the first. With the girder the entire fork assembly moves against a rigid spring. Of the three systems, glide, springer, and girder, only the springer is suited to modifying the front end a radical amount.

When a front end is lengthened any amount, it will tend to rotate the entire bike upward above the rear-wheel-axle centerline. This will raise the center of gravity, and increase wheelbase a slight amount. However, most chopper builders are after an extended wheelbase primarily. This can be accomplished either by extending the frame in the neck area by a few inches, or raking the neck.

Neck rake merely means the angle of the steering head in relation to a fixed plane. Some people measure this relative to a horizontal line drawn through the neck, others relative to a vertical line. The majority of chopper enthusiasts prefer all measurements to be made from the vertical.

The angle of the steering head, or neck, will have a direct effect on how the motorcycle handles under certain conditions. A bicycle has a very small amount of neck angle, which makes it easy to turn at slow speeds. However, bicycles used for high-speed racing will have a greater neck angle (the neck will lay down more) as this will make the bike go in a straight line better at higher speeds. The same is true for motorcycles. Speedway racers built for extremely short, circular race tracks have practically no neck angle. They are easy to throw into foot-dragging turns, but very difficult to steer in a straight line. Bonneville motorcycles have a very high neck angle for high-speed stability, but would be practically impossible to ride on the street. Somewhere between those extremes are the angles used by chopper builders.

Again, the experts generally agree that any neck rake, or angle from the vertical, greater than 40 degrees is excessive. A stock production motorcycle is likely to have an angle of between 25 and 30 degrees. It is possible to buy custom chopper frames with the additional 10-degree rack already included. Should you have a stock frame modified,

**195**

it would be a good idea to have the area Magnafluxed. This process, available in practically every community, usually through a machine or welding shop, is a form of metal X-ray. It will show any cracks in the metal or weld that might fail later. Keep your X-ray certificate to show the motor-vehicle department, too.

The characteristics of front-end geometry are simple, although most people try to make a mystery of them. When you rake the neck, you increase the angle of the steering head, and this in turn increases a thing called trail. An increase in trail is the factor that causes low-speed handling and turnnig difficulties. For instance, when a glide front end is used with a raked neck, there is no way to reduce trail.

Stand off to the side of a front end and visualize a vertical line passing through the front axle. Now consider a line going through the center of the neck, downward at an angle, to the ground. The distance apart between these two lines on the ground is trail (the vertical spot "trails," or is behind, the angle line spot). The greater this distance, the more the front end will tend to "flop over" when the wheel is moved out of a straight position.

The custom front end uses a set of brackets from the rigid part of a springer fork. The springing part of the fork connects to these brackets, allowing them to move up and down, and the axle is connected farther ahead. But the custom fork builders have considered a possibility of a 40-degree neck rake, and have positioned the axle so the total trail is approximately 2 inches. Obviously a rigid front end, or one that has no springing action at all (which makes it similar to an extended glide setup), will have an even greater trail and be difficult to control.

When a front end is modified, a smaller-diameter wheel and tire is usually advised, as this will make control easier. Often builders go to a narrow tire in preference to the stock wide type.

It is possible to buy practically everything you need to build a chopper at the local bike shop, but then the very essence of personal design is lost. Special talents can also be sought, such as frame molders and custom painters. The more work you do yourself (and on a motorcycle it is considerably more easy than on a car), the greater will be your pride in the finished product.

Most customizers stay out of performance equipment for the engine until the bike has been on the road for a while and all the chassis bugs have been sorted out. That isn't necessarily a prerequisite, though, and anyone living in the cold climates may want to take advantage of long downtime to put some suds into the engine. As with hot rods, the secret to outstanding engine performance is careful selection of speed equipment, and thorough installation.

A final note of caution. Before starting on any chopper project, it is wise to check with local chopper builders on state vehicle equipment laws and law interpretation. In the past some states actually created laws designed to discourage modifications. In these cases experience showed the states were hasty with poorly structured laws, and chopper enthusiasts were able to get the laws changed after long effort. Some states, though, still have rather arbitrary attitudes about any type of modified motorcycle.

Before sinking $250 in a premium square springer fork assembly, it would be nice to know if such a system will be passed by law enforcement. Building within the framework of existing laws is easier than bucking the tide.

The chopper has been a good part of motorcycle history, when taken in the context of anything modified, and it is likely to become even more important in American motorcycling during coming years. Like hot rodding, it will be a continually changing sport, which is the reason for its great popularity. A chopper is for anyone with imagination.

# Index

# Index

Spark arrestors, 64, 148
Spark plugs, checking, 45, 76
Sportster, 161-162, 166, 187, 188
Springers, 194
Sprockets, 38, 91, 97, 99, 100, 101, 104, 105-107
Starters, electric, 33
"SuperGlide," 162-163, 182
Suzuki, 11, 60, 120, 163, 188

Theft problem, 30-31
Timing, 78
Tires, 124-138
  checking, 39-40
  mini-bike, 180
Touring bikes, see Road bikes
Track bikes, 14
Trade-in agreement, 159
Trail, 196
Trail bikes, 6, 106, 139-149, 150
Transmission fluid, 95, 99

Transmissions, 89-107
Trials events, 151-152, 154
Triumph, 8, 53, 155, 166, 185
Trouble-shooting, 72-83
Tuning, 71-88
  chassis, 71
  exhaust, 72
  intake ram, 72
  performance, 71
  power, 72

Used bikes, fixing up, 35-49

Valve work, 67

Wheels, 124-138
*Wild Ones, The* (movie), 183
Wiring, examination of, 41-45, 73
Wolfmueller & Geisenhof firm, 4

Yamaha, 11, 64, 120, 163

## DATE DUE

| | | | |
|---|---|---|---|
| NOV 24 '75 | AG 6 '84 | MAY 9 '95 | |
| MAR 2 '76 | NO 26 '85 | | |
| MAR 17 '76 | DE 31 '85 | | |
| APR 6 '76 | AP 17 '86 | | |
| JUN 10 '76 | MR 28 '87 | | |
| JUN 28 '76 | UG 3 | | |
| OCT 3 '76 | E 24 '91 | | |
| DEC 20 '76 | FB 6 | | |
| JUN 20 '77 | MR 13 '92 | | |
| JUL 8 '77 | AG 07 08 | | |
| AUG 22 '77 | | | |
| FEB 6 '78 | | | |
| Mar 28 | | | |
| FEB 20 '79 | | | |
| DE 31 '81 | | | |
| OC 7 '82 | | | |
| MR 19 '83 | | | |
| JA 30 '84 | | | |

GAYLORD                                          PRINTED IN U.S.A.